Lyn Hejinian

POSI-
TIONS
OF THE
SUN

Belladonna*
Germinal Texts 2

POSITIONS

for
LMO
all night
and
every day

OF THE SUN
Introduction, John Keene.....5

Positions of the Sun

POSITIONS

John Keene
INTRODUCTION

As 2018 hurtles towards its end, the US remains mired in a series of wars, in the Middle East, in Africa, in South Asia, perhaps in spots across the globe that remain opaque except to the commander in chief, military, and military-industrial complex. Other US wars ——— of capital and finance, of ideology and belief, against science and truth, among others ——— persist as well, shifting in shape and size. These often-interlinked conflicts have spanned so many decades that concepts such as "state of emergency," "state of exception," and "perpetual war" are hardly literary, scientific, or philosophical fancies. Just as the country has heard more than once that any given war has concluded, that a given opponent has been "defeated," another enemy or phalanx of enemies arises. These endless wars exact psychologically and materially traumatic tolls that we have barely come to terms with.

One especially severe moment in the war of capital occurred a decade ago, when the US suffered the worst economic crisis since the Great Depression of the 1930s and 1940s. This calamity, widely known as the "Great Recession," unfolded in 2007, the last full year of George W. Bush's presidency, and began with an accelerating string of bank failures. This cataclysm would eventually include massive numbers of home foreclosures, business failures and mass layoffs, and a cratering of the US economy, spreading virally to encompass nearly every major economy across the globe. Yet only six months into Barack Obama's presidency, in June 2009, after several rounds of bailouts of many of the economic crisis's chief agents in the financial industry, an array of economists, including the nonpartisan National Bureau of Economic Research, proclaimed that the Great Recession had ended, despite its evident lingering effects. The positive economic indicators belied the social and political crises, exacerbated by neoliberal policies and regimes of austerity, that still impact the US and the rest of the world today.

With Positions, poet, essayist and translator Lyn Hejinian continues her dialogue with those writers who have directly and indirectly taken up the topic of endless war and the 2007-9 economic crisis and its devastating aftermath, through a narrative that also can be read as a lyric phenomenology. In 26 chapters, with a Coda, each corresponding to a two-week period in the economic crisis's wake, and cycling through real and imagined characters engaging in a variety of forms of critique and dissent, Hejinian shows (as she had in prior works such as the multiple versions of My Life, Writing Is an Aid to Memory, and Oxota: A Short Russian Novel, to name just a few of her books) how to write, and thus orient, a critical aesthetic vision in relation to the society around oneself and of which one is also an integral part. This is a text of discovery and uncovering, in which these fragments of everyday human experience do not just metonymically reflect our society's complexities, but reveal the differences and harmonies within it.

Hejinian invites us into this world through her propulsively associative prose, making legible expressions of a consciousness, singular at any moment, collective over Positions' span, which is always seeking, ever in motion. The characters ——— and the narrative itself ——— engage in the individual and collaborative labor of dreaming, perceiving, reading, citing, talking, and making. To put it another way, and to contrast it to conventional forms of realist fiction or lyric poetry, this text itself, in its forward advance, aims to embody collective perception and action, even when it at times falters or must double back on itself. What becomes material are the turns and turnings, of thought and critique, in words, rendering visible the intertextual weave of discourse from which this and any narrative emerges, and the futurity it makes possible.

Currents of art, politics, history, and literary, social and cultural criticism course through and constitute Positions' narrative. The text's critical polyphony is grounded in the quotidian and the contingent, much like the passage of the sun and its effects the title itself refers to. Immersed in this book, the reader may feel simultaneously seated in a room carefully peering over a shoulder, perusing one of the many texts Hejinian evokes and quotes, while also standing amid an Oakland or Berkeley throng holding signs and placards, hovering behind barricades or in a space set aside for organizing, eavesdropping on the casual and familiar chitchat of fellow activists. One result of this juxtaposition is to suggest a connection between positions, foregrounding the potential for a both/and scenario within the larger biopolitical scenario, in which the life of the mind and the life of struggle are not opposed, but mutually reinforcing.

Above all, though, Positions is a demonstration of Hejinian's distinctive skill as an innovator in poetry and prose. Reading this book, one may have the sense that each sentence, phrase or fragment has been hasped to the one preceding it and the one following it almost effortlessly to produce sensations of surprise and recognition. Yet Hejinian also allows the prose's seams to show, letting the abrupt collisions at the level of idea, sound, imagery, and figuration, occur as they will. Positions possesses the depth and amplitude of a heftier text, and wading in, the reader quickly encounters the sensation of immersion in a world that, in its particularities, exists primarily in these pages, but which mirrors the society in which this text appears. To quote Hejinian:

> We live amidst and, however unconsciously, partake in constellations of the real that cultural standards, narrative givens, etc. can't make sense of, or even perceive. Simply to realize they are here, emitting flickers from the feathery increments of their iridescent half-lives, requires the kinds of time that we are rarely, if ever, permitted to have. (53)

Among its many gifts, Positions presents us those constellations of the real and the evanescent flickers they bear. It grounds us in the language and time we want and need and, here, are allowed to grapple with and revel in.

April 2008 ——— July 2015

1

The sun is rising. Chuk-a-chuka-chuk, chuka-chuk, chuka-chuk. How we love it! The petals of the sun flare, waver, bend, spin. Someone sings. Light comes through a window, falls across a plate, illuminates the mottled surface of a shark's tooth, a small red pocketknife. Humans are forever creating new allegories out of things they find in the world. A feather, a paper flag on a stick, and an ivory chopstick are stuck beside an upright tulip in a jar. Evidently someone has combed a rubbish heap, reevaluated some bits of debris, plucked them out of the limbo they'd drifted into when stripped of context, given them another moment. Aesthetic recontextualization brings things to a temporary halt, which is different from the false halt to which decontextualization had brought them. Somewhere in the neighborhood a dog is barking, saying unmistakably, "Hurt, hurt ——— hurt, hurt ——— hurt, hurt ——— hurt, hurt ——— hurt, hurt." It speaks in iambic pentameter. Heavy clouds had promised rain the sky could not deliver to a motley group in uniform, the pigeons moaning in the eaves, the new year's sun now free and clear. The conversion of what was the neighborhood pharmacy into a café and bookstore has begun with demolition. From the southwest corner of the street comes the shriek of crowbars wrenching out lathes, the thunder of a sledgehammer smashing plaster, clouds of dust. The workers, all wearing protective masks, are indistinguishable from one another, carrying rubble out of the building, tossing broken furniture, glass, ruined merchandise into the back of a truck. Perhaps memory will take this all in and intensify it. According to Michel de Certeau, memory in its ancient sense "designates a presence to the plurality of times and is thus not limited to the past." That's lucky. In time of war people resign themselves to prodigious extinctions with dusty bravura. "Who taught surgery to primates?" exclaims Ravi; the question is posed rhetorically. Commando shrugs his shoulder. "Your move." How heavy-handed we are! The sunlight pushes into the trees which, moving in the breeze, seem to be trying to avoid it ———— or to shake it off. We can't assume that behind the stories everywhere unfolding, secrets exist that require interpretation. Lives are practices, saying just enough of what they do. Some people dream, some lie about their childhood which was so uneventful that, as if it were tall grass or thick weeds, things fell into it and were lost. Some are always looking for an orchid to add to their collection. Some accumulate explanations for their vague but persistent perturbations. And some foresee infestation. "What if I'm cut off midway through a joke or confession?" "What if, because no bee bothers, I'm unable to contribute my share to the collective pollination?" No one has kept count of the bowls of oatmeal we've consumed, the number of English muffin halves we've spread with marmalade and consumed while reading the daily newspaper whose headline fonts have recently been enlarged (or "updated," as a reporter puts it, making news of the change in the look of the news), and whose pages today give orchestral treatment to the retrospective agony of a "grieving populace": "Firefighters lit the grill and worked the room...." But mortality imposes on us the inability to help the people we care about after we are dead. This is, in a social sense, what defines mortality. The immortality of the ancient gods, meanwhile ———— which is to say, their existence ———— was made known to people of their times precisely through their intercession in people's affairs. The wounded, meanwhile ———— are they not, like the elderly, a site of accumulated time? Or are they something that time has passed through, as a wind passes through a tree, breaking limbs, tattering leaves, bending its branches, and leaving it behind? The officers are functional equivalents of capitalists. They are about to invest troops in a project for which they are trying to find a name. Gemini Vitae! Headwater Spree! Enduring Handhold! Omniscient Dawn! A teenage girl appears on the overpass, carrying a crying baby in one arm and holding a somber child by the hand. Behind them two mangled cars, one of them smoking, lie smashed against a guardrail. For just a moment, simultaneously, both the child and the teenager begin to wail, but they recover instantly and walk silently away. Tolstoy? Trotsky? They both gave a great deal of attention to educational theories and practices, foreseeing a necessity to revolutionize minds. The passion for coalition, conspiracy, and forging communities is, according to Charles Fourier, "such an imperious need... that if it cannot satisfy itself in real intrigues, it will seek out artificial ones like games, the theater, or novels." A rampage has occurred, carried out by a "homegrown terrorist" or perhaps a "troubled veteran" or a "disgruntled former employee" ——— in the news accounts of it, different captions are slid into place, others are withdrawn. On the third page of the newspaper is a photograph of three young men and one young woman in pale camouflage floating silently past an airport newsstand on the terminal's moving walkway. The caption below it reads, "Being there has always been inherent to the experience of architecture." Time proves that the imagination makes many inappropriate comparisons. A vast stretch of sky lies between a few scattered, ambiguous clouds. The sun illuminates more than the foreground, it shines on the buildings or bushes in the background, on the picnickers or shoppers or front yard grasses or power lines. It may be that the landscape is dreamy. "Sleep," as Victor Hugo has said, "has a close relationship with the possible." In the middle drawer of the wooden bureau in the bedroom Tamarind Magee finds the black V-neck cardigan sweater she wants to wear over her flannel pajama top and short red skirt, and under it a package of Trojan© "Intense"© condoms, Webster's Compact Rhyming Dictionary, blue-tinted shades, and a half-pound of T. E. Lawrence Desert Oasis© trail mix in a Ziploc© baggie. There's a trio of swinging gates to negotiate, one of painted wood, one of chicken wire stapled across a simple wooden frame, and the third is painted yellow and made of corrugated metal, but the way to it is barred by a pair of cats who face her, ears back, fur bristling, and teeth bared. "I totally want to see this," Tamarind Magee says eagerly, in a spirit of unambiguous camaraderie in the dark with Ravi Abedourian. Traumatized soldiers coming home from war experience a recurrent return, the fluttering of a totality from which there's only sporadic relief. The world in its entirety as they have experienced it remains wholly the same, spread out across time as something that is always subject to already known incursions of unpredictably occurring violence, fear, and pain. Life takes place in terms of a perpetual arrival before an impenetrable wall around a monument to their experiences that they can't reach. Their attempts to accept the still persuasive but now irredeemably altered fiction of originality, of the entirely contemporary and unprecedented, the fiction of the thing of the moment, come to a halt ——— the false halt that is the purely present moment. Jeanie Johnson presses the pencil point deep into the paper, she engraves the head of a graphite horse on the page, the side of her hand leaves smudges along the paper's bottom edge. She wants the drawing to be sculptural, urban, able to claim its place on the streets among the hard objects made of metal, glass, plastic, or rock. Jeanie Johnson's way of knowing things is to add to them, to supervene. Milk cartons yield, goldfish cower, motorcycles pull away, the cardboard nest and bundled belongings of a homeless woman take over a doorway with a kitten on her winter clothing in possession. With respect to the passing of minutes, few of us have much in common. Men and women in the supermarket battle for goods but also for time. They pilfer lemons, then abandon full shopping cars; they jab pencils into the shrink-wrapped cheese, then knowingly pay too much for frostbitten artichokes. Situations are the product of circulation, some of it purposeless and unproductive, the rest furthering growth, filling experience, generating events, bringing things to their terminus; life at any given moment is a composite of situations. Some of them form impediments, blocking circulation. Even under normal circumstances, everyday life is subject to restrictions. Les sorgueurs vont sollicer des gails à la lune. Of this bit of 19th-century street argot, Victor Hugo remarks, "This sweeps past the mind like a flock of specters. We do not know what we are seeing." Translated into standard English, it says, "The prowlers are going to steal some horses tonight." But why the standard English? Why not something quite apart from fiction, something that might easily be true: "Lollipops will solace some little girls by moonlight." People are experiencing grief ——— it can be described as a persistent single grief (susceptible to description as "dull," "sharp," "nagging," "radiating," etc.) or as a sequence of separate griefs (each experienced for the terrible first time, each a shocking occurrence that would previously have been considered impossible). In time, consciously or not, the grieving find that they are watching to see when the grief, or which grief, will go the farthest. They no longer clearly remember what has brought on the grief ———— nor when or where it began. It belongs to the world of the habitual: getting up, answering the phone, reheating pea soup. It is inextricably a part of the world of dutifulness, obedience. In the airport terminal, travelers converse: This one is apple-flavored, it tastes like, the numbers are all wrong, also looking for a party of two, Zimbabwe is pretty much like Texas, it's like it's always Owners Day, you stand for your nephew? The young widow watching the tarmac doesn't want to tell her story but she wants it known, she wants the feel of it realized, but maybe, she thinks, as the Pleiades are, peripherally, momentarily, there's no release of nostalgia possible from it. The things we see ———— wow, some of them aren't even there! The war needs an index: Addiction to, Alternatives to, Approval ratings of, Arguments for, Battle cries in, Camaraderie in, Censorship during, Cessation of, Children in, Conditions during, Cowardice in, Declaration of, Department of, Economic repercussions of, Environmental effects of, Expenses of, Faces of, Fallen in, False peace during, Fear of, Funding for, Growing resistance to, Heightened security during, Heroes of, Hostilities during, Human cost of, Human proclivity for, Ideological underpinnings of, Inevitability of, Losers of, Media coverage of, Mental health problems following, Preliminaries to, Prisoners of, Profits from, Protestors against, Public understandings of, Racism as, Ravages of, Shifting definitions of, Sites of, Soldiers in, Spread of, Stages of, State of, Structures of, Territorial ambitions behind, Traditions of, Training for, Victims of, Weapons of, Winners of, Women in. See also War crimes, War dead, War games, War heroes, War injuries, War memorials, War resisters, War shortages, War stories, War toys, War tribunals, War zones. See also Capitalist wars, Ideological wars, Drug wars, Global wars, Local wars, Undeclared wars, World wars. In an allegorical world, everything is connected to everything else. Pow-pow ———— we fight for the sun.

<blockquote>
It is
immune to exegesis and therefore beloved
and promises to speak the truth like a desert ————
</blockquote>

2

Baudelaire called the public, in its wild enthusiasm for photography, "sun-worshippers." They loved what they saw. "From that moment onward, our loathsome society rushed, like Narcissus, to contemplate its trivial image on the metallic plate." Here is a photograph of a building in ruins. The caption reads "Victoriously." This is a politically devastated landscape and, although very differently, a politically charged photo. We can see a child's shovel and pail in the foreground and some seashells beside them. And we can see a "Vacancy" sign in a window of a building off to the right of the ruins. The photographer may be obsessed with death, or with fending it off. They are not the same thing. The landscape is stark, but the rubble is minutely textured, purveying pattern. Photography is perhaps the first of the Enlightenment arts, utilizing the technology that the Enlightenment's anthropocentric view of creation assumes and fulfilling some of its not entirely false promises. The photo-loving public can have its shadows, rendered believable, prolonged indefinitely, and even immortalized. Photos can contribute to the aesthetics of minutiae, with their promise of infinitude. Attention to the miniscule (which has provided science with its own province of sublimity) might stand as a counter to a concomitant awareness of orders of magnitude that include atrocity, war, capitalism, and perhaps ———— though it may be mortality's saving grace ———— death. Indeed, photography enthusiasts might be better described as worshippers of shadows, after-images, history. Even large format photographs ———— as in Doug Hall's magnificent digital C-print works, some measuring as much as 4 by 5 feet ———— seem more immediate (though, paradoxically, less intimate) than paintings. For intimate encounters we turn to time. It is there that we feel the intimacy of other lives and others' experiences of things. True, as progenitor of the objective sciences, the Enlightenment can hardly be deemed a wellspring of intimacy. Forget the selfie! I'm doing my best not to contribute to the cult of surveillance. But, by bringing the objectifiable world home, so to speak, the Enlightenment did, to some extent, increase the human capacity for intimate experience ———— that is, for experiencing things intimately, and hence inconclusively. Adorno, writing about the late poetry of Hölderlin, speaks of inconclusiveness as an instrument of "the paratactic revolt against synthesis." "Hölderlin," he says, "so transmutes the form of unity that not only is multiplicity reflected within it ———— that is possible within traditional synthetic language as well ———— but in addition the unity indicates that it knows itself to be inconclusive." Within the dark interior of the camera is an hallucinating eye enchanted by the passing image of an emotional face or pigeons circling under the sky. It sees things one can't discern sufficiently and that are on their way to expiration, but the way is so long as to be unimaginable except as an instantaneous, blazing flash in an otherwise soft black depth that isn't a space but a plunging of space too dark and empty to see as anything at all. One can't look directly at the sun, either, of course; everything one has forgotten is in it. Near a set of keys, a hammer lies on the table beside a paper napkin. A stuffed animal ———— a brown nubbled dog with splay and floppy limbs ———— on its side in a chair; over the back of the chair a black leather jacket is draped. This is yet another in a sequence of winter "spare the air" days. The branches of the street trees (plum, gingko, sycamore, birch) are leafless, but the yellow flowers of creeping woodsorrel are blooming in front yards, median strips, and weed beds. There's a used teabag on the napkin, surrounded by an ochre stain. The newspaper carries an inky, uncontroversial image of Martin Luther King Jr., photographed against an indistinct background. It's the annual tribute. The expression on King's face blocks interpretation, or, rather, that is exactly what he's expressing: resistance to interpretation. The story of everyday life (repetition) proceeds slowly. The story of young QJ takes his entire lifetime to unfold.

Streets all around us like jawbones
bringing marvels that rival a robin's
and that's real 'cause both are so common
———— so common, so come on, so common ....

Carlotta snaps her fingers. "Feelin!" she says. "Playing music's useless," says Diego; "that's what's good about it." "I don't think it's useless!" QJ brings both drumsticks down on the high-hat, the right slightly before the left. "Streets all around us like jawbones. Lot a things like that, around us like jawbones. Gives me a chance to express myself." "I'd say what you express is that you like to beat on things," says Carlotta. "Fuck, playing this shit is useful," says Flip. "Like how?" Didier Padilla Brown is hastily tuning his guitar ———— pong pong, pang pang, ping ping ———— the harmonics match. He swings, strums, bends, kicks. It is said of him that he has one eye too many, prompting one pungent critic to comment that it is an irrelevance since Didier keeps it closed. It's an improviser's eye. He turns it on the kids. "Listen up." Didier Brown values spontaneity, outbursts, "best after years of practice," he says. Everything about the past is to be remembered; "boundaries exist so you can pound on them," he says, "and the first beat's not the one you're going to hear." A helicopter passes noisily overhead, generally following Telegraph Avenue north toward Berkeley on its way to drift over the early rush hour traffic, locate a criminal, or hover over a protest. "What you are witnessing is the beginning of the end of civil society." The helicopters compete for the acoustic space, cops loiter on the fringes of the crowd, one leans against a sycamore tree. Now and then within the circuitries of communication the volume of noise increases, sometimes aspiring to cause interference, sometimes aspiring to overcome it. Take this little poem of Lyn Hejinian's, for example:

> wilt
>   unnamed button
> store it all

The tercet is spare, but incautious. Its very brevity inflates it. It seems peremptory, or irascible. It is certainly not gnomic; it is not trying to hold any of its energy in reserve. It has a strongly expressive quality; something has excited emotion, but just what that something is or was and what that emotion (or complex of emotions) is remains unclear. But clarity is, obviously, not the point. That said, clarity seems even less the point in P.

Inman's chapbook <u>Ocker</u>. It is either semantically protean or in ruins, radically inconclusive or beyond repair.

> oneitd , crine
> mend zin

Perhaps the forces of history have ravaged the words and phrases of the poem, so that what we have are only its embattled, allegorical, fierce remains, or we are witness to those words and phrases coming into formation. The poem presents us with something that might have been said or that might be said yet. Gertrude Stein claims that masterpieces "exist because they came to be as something that is an end in itself." In this respect, she says, they are "opposed to the business of living which is relation and necessity." Young lovers imagine their love to be just such a masterpiece. As Kierkegaard's pseudonymous B puts it, "The lovers are deeply convinced that in itself their relationship is a complete whole that will never be changed." But it seems whole because it feels incontrovertible, inevitable: "Romantic love manifests itself as immediate by exclusively resting in natural necessity...." The same could be said of existence ——— one comes into being from natural necessity, but in this case it's less an inevitability than through circumstantial fortune. The sequences of events resulting in a birth are multiple, their sequentiality largely inadvertent, and perhaps from only one of them might a birth have been reasonably predicted ——— though any particular one couldn't have been predicted at all. And, even when a child might have been intended, the child was not itself a participant in the intention. But soon it will have to realize that it exists. The Uzbek poet Muhammad Salikh has credited that realization to one's shadow. "I am a very young child," he says. "That's the dream." He says he is flying high above the desert. He swoops through the air, his shadow racing to the left, then to the right, sometimes shrinking into a valley or dry riverbed, sometimes burgeoning on top of the dunes. He wants to stay in the sky forever, teasing his shadow. Suddenly, far below him, he sees his mother standing in the desert. He lands beside her, and she takes his hand. He tries to pull away. "Come fly," he says, but his mother points to his feet. His shadow has caught him and holds him to the sand. "That is how I was born," Salikh said. One's shadow does more than supply one with a caption. The allegorical comes affixed to remnants of the past of which it speaks, but it can speak only incompletely and cryptically of the lost whole (its true and proper time) ———— this is a point that Walter Benjamin makes ————whereas the shadow can extend into the future, and condense itself into the present, as well as come out of the dark. Spinach frigate and ledger cello and churlish Lily Ball and dysfunctional ephemera and puppetry and fusion flautist Samantha Bell Chow. For the most part, I myself am not afraid of chaos but of fending it off: the tedious work, the interminable sense of obligation, the compelling call to return over and over again to the defense of a regimen of familiarity, and of predictability, which runs counter to everyday life (repeating repetition). Drowsily timeless colossus and lowercase pictography and pasta puttanesca and rain, at last. It's hard to discern where history breaks off and everyday life (implacable repetition) begins. But what about this? Near the Oakland MAP a church is being demolished, the boards are being pried from the studs, carefully stacked, incrementally hauled away, presumably to be reused. The graceful, though somewhat squat, arched windows, empty of panes (which were of plain, not stained, glass), having been removed, lean against the side of a truck. The reader is not apt to read this as a speculative passage, she is likely instead to take it as straightforward description, accurate to what it purports to represent, even if what it presents is local to a fiction and redolent with interpretation. What about this: The hills rising at the eastern edge of the urban area provide a perspectival panoply, while to the west the bay offers an endless prospect, a scintillating distance. One wide ugly avenue is the only major street running between them; uninviting squat commercial buildings, cheap motels, copy shops, and then a stretch of Indian restaurants and a cluster of sari shops line it from end to end. Or this: A man approaches, his feet and legs encased in armor made of shining silver scales. The front edges of his armored boots are decorated with curling silver claws much as the prow of a ship might bear a masthead in the form of a nymph whose long curls blow out over the waves. Each element of the work, every particular, exists as a point of encounter, rather than of separability; each particular serves as an intersection, a portal, a source of energy, and a point of departure (rather than terminus). In his old age, the writer James Earl French says he no longer has the energy to express his ideas, his greatest pleasure now is in getting new ones and he acquires them with a sense of urgency, he reads, he takes notes, I'll never do anything with them, he says. He has lost interest in depicting the world as it appears to him; he has lost his interest in offering his particular, peculiar perspective on things. I want to know the world as it is, not as I see it, he says, but how is it? "That question's not so obviously political," says Jean Day, "maybe not political at all." Reality ——— the given ——— is the problem that constrains objectivity, prompting withdrawal. "Impoverished sense is the real problem," Jean says, brushing her right hand gently in the air as if to move the statement aside. But of course everything is imminent in anything, with corresponding troubles and vexations, things in need of attention, bringing many bits that concern us, their pertinent worries and the accompanying worrying. Time gets intersected by the comings and goings of its dramatis personae: truck driver, short order cook, oncology nurse, barista, florist, bank teller, dog walker, student, civil rights lawyer, electrician, figment of imagination. Real shadows are subject to the time of day, and to the position of the sun. What does one do with the excitement one feels when in one's excitement one becomes exciting and excites awareness of the excitement and the exciting? And for how long can one do it?

3

I can't concentrate for long ———— I can't properly and significantly focus ———— on a source of worry or anxiety or fear without moving off mentally, and sometimes physically too; in just such a way, too, I change position when I wake from a nightmare so as to turn away from the site of distress. I'm hit by emotional heat ———— sorrow, shame, fear. I want to kick my back, my neck. I want to kick you. Be forgettable and be forgotten, you sunk bog tromper, soggy runner, unformed rotten woman in quicksand! Leave me alone! As one turns, one asserts one's autonomy, one distinguishes oneself. But in doing so one allies oneself with the unhappier forces of irony, utilizing irony's propensity to deracinate materials from their meanings. One becomes a mere fragment of one's own history. Maybe fragmentation is the condition that Cordelia wants to prevent when Lear poses his nightmarish challenge to his daughters. Lear invites his daughters to gain <u>private</u> autonomy for themselves through sacrifice of the <u>common</u> autonomy, a kingdom. But Cordelia's love for her father is bound to that kingdom, as it can't help but be, since it entails for her the entirety of the known world. No single expression and no amount of expressing can speak of her world, or of her knowing it. The linearity of language cannot bear it. Its syntax would shatter. And so Cordelia cannot enter into the dividing up of the world that Lear demands and that her speaking would bring about. Nonetheless, tragically, her reserve does so. She refuses to memorialize what belongs properly to the ever-changing active life of remembering. Out of insolently casual quotidian living into cautious obligatory history, Cordelia is precipitated into the situation of a mourner. And so she becomes an historian, bound to an imperative to remember. But if, as some argue, aesthetic experience is at its best when it most closely approximates immediacy ———— of perception, of response, of feeling, of that mode of understanding that isn't cognitive but, rather, transmutes experience into meaningfulness (sometimes almost bypassing meaning, in the epistemological sense, altogether) —————— it has to eschew remembering. Lear wants to arrange conditions for himself that will allow him the leisurely, regressive aesthetic pleasure of forgetting —————— hence his desire for a declaration of love from his daughters, the verbal equivalent of a memorial. Or a list. The semantic temporality (which I'm inclined to term the paratactic present) of paratactic attention is closely akin to that of Gertrude Stein's "beginning again and again": we come to one thing and another in a moment to moment place to place sequence and series of experiences experienced without any necessary or determining order, their details appearing in such a way as to make one conscious of them and to assure that they "never," as Adorno puts it, "merge tracelessly into the totality." This is the syntax of forgetting in a semantics of remembering, its units askew, vivid, and half unhinged. Shot of a dry landscape, a small group of people standing on a bluff, hands clasped and heads turned to the sky, fissured by a bolt of lightning. Shot of a city at night in rain, dark streets gleaming, some cars, tall buildings. Shot of a great bank of blue-white ice hissing and crumbling at sea's edge. Shot of two women fighting, one holding a knife in her raised hand, with a table under a white tablecloth in the foreground on which rests a bowl of peaches and blackberries. Shot of a flirtatious child; he's pretending to shoot me (with his finger) and I pretend to die, followed by a second shot in which he revives me by sweeping his arms outward from his chest and waggling his fingers at me. Beaming child. A plot emerges. This one needs only another bolt of lightning to become allegorical. Sequentiality is a structure; the sequence of shots frames the world. Or do they issue a warning? A propensity for list-making, which is not atypical of the superstitious, is frightening for the paranoid. It reassures the superstitious that she can exercise a modicum of control over the phenomenological ceaselessness of the world; it gives expression to a perceived orderliness without imposing order on things. But the paranoid reads into the list and finds evidence in it that nefarious forces have been assembled and are at work in all the reaches of her world. The allegorical can be viewed either (as in the case of the superstitious) as manifesting continuity and homogeneity across differences or (as with the paranoid) as manifesting discontinuity and heterogeneity across similarities. Listing is generally an evaluative activity, holding life at bay. In that case, it probably doesn't have any aesthetic value, despite whatever satisfactions or emotional excitements it generates. In the Phaedrus, Socrates warns against writing, lest the written replace the remembered: "If men learn this, it will implant forgetfulness in their souls; they will cease to exercise memory because they rely on that which is written, calling things to remembrance no longer from within themselves, but by means of external marks. What you have discovered is a recipe not for memory, but for reminder." But Socrates might have said something else, viz.: If clocks time this, it will transplant chaos from our spirits; they will hasten to prohibit spontaneity because they are bound to whatever is legislated, luring things to prison no longer from outside themselves, but by virtue of inner proclivities. What we have created is the prospect not of horizons but of fences. Or perhaps he might have said this: If signals seize this, it will verify tyranny in our society; they will hurry to captivate consumers because they relay onward that which is obscured, culling things from history no longer from behind them but obliterated by splattered signs. What they have established is a record not of happiness but of greed. Humans are incessantly noisy. They talk as they eat, they chatter as they window-shop, they shout as they dance, they blather as they telephone, they yell as they brush their hair, they mutter as they look in the mirror, they laugh and sing and shriek and call as they bask or shovel or sauté or shower. I dream that I am praised for my sentences ——— or, to be more precise, for my evident interest in sentences. The evidence of your interest, says an appreciative authority, is in the sentences. I don't know how to respond in the dream except vivaciously. Assembling words and phrases is what poets do, after all; that's what generates ideas and images, representations and messages and depictions, whose substance is often different from (and sometimes indifferent to) the poet's desires and intentions. Suddenly, as if to be remembered, as if out of accumulated fragments of perception but in fact out of dictionaries and the ongoing babble of the brain, something comes abruptly into view, an assemblage that is textual ——— sudden, perhaps fleeting, never complete.

It is also very likely to be wrong. The errors that inform each memory impinge on everything that's remembered; reality is simply its fringe effect, like the visages that drift like mist from the edges of a late painting by Bonnard. They mark the moment at which the lyric "I" pauses to speak to the lyric "you."

> O you who are the sum of summits,
> You,
> Chief, president, boss, chairperson, czar
> And admiral of my elbows,
> My pilot and navigator, chauffeur
> And capitan,
> You, o receiver of terms of endearment and irritation
> > that I improvise, invent, and apply to you and to
> > no one else,
> O you, ...

And so on. With indexical lyricism the poet begins to pet, and occasionally poke, her beloved. Such violence is characteristic of the lyric poem ———— and why? Because feelings must be powerfully moved, so that they are shaken out of their well-worn grooves. I have written a twelve-part, twelve-page poem. The lines, of varying length, are placed at varying distances from the margins; each page becomes a landscape formed by the thoughts/phrases scattered across it. I read over each section one last time, stamping the pages as I approve them with a single word in block caps: DECEASED. We dream unshared experiences in an unshareable world, no longer in a realm of beings acting and speaking together. "New Yorkers are all provincial," says Lei-lei Wilson Tin to Tamarind Magee. "Not that anyone cares," says Lily Ball with muted malice. "New York would be dope." Commando pinches a slice of pepperoni off the pizza on the platter in front of them. "I'm thinking of writing a graphic biography," says Lei-lei. "Of whom?" "Of the woman my mother wants me to become." "Grim," says Tamarind Magee. As Charlie Altieri notes, in the course of an eloquent analysis of the culturally-impotent characters in James Joyce's Dubliners: "We realize in retrospect why the children in their disappointment become the adults who disappoint." All that's left for the disappointed children, whose options are limited from the very start, is to find an identity that can bolster them enough to allow them psychically to survive, if not to flourish, in the milieu to which their lives are consigned. And that iden‐ tity ——— the one most readily available and probably the only one anywhere in sight ——— is that of the disappointing (dis‐ appointer) adults. The child by now is, in her disappointment, angry, but at herself. She has become not only the focus of dis‐ appointment but an embodiment of disappointment. She is a failure in a world of the failed and failing. "My dad's a creep," says Tamarind Magee. "Seems like you get off on hating him," says Lily Ball. For months embarrassment has angered Tamarind Magee, now anger embarrasses her. She shuts up. As a honey bee circles a clump of garden sage, it defecates. Something like thought ——— a polyphonic awareness ——— crosses its flight path. In a previous life as a human it was obedient except when crossed. In its next life, as an azalea ——— a life it doesn't fore‐ see ——— it will no longer entertain thoughts of revenge.

4

Lorine Niedecker handwrote her poem "Paean to Place," one stanza per page, into a four-by-six-inch autograph book, which she then presented to a friend. Kit Robinson composed his "Ice Cubes," one word per line, in his head. Roofers on a neighbor's house are talking, sometimes shouting, to each other in Spanish. I hear the ongoing crescendo-cadenced conversation, and also a dog, whining, a subdued low urban roar, a bird, singing, a flushing toilet. I take it all in, additions to the bourgeois inward-ness that I learned from early childhood to value. As a child, like my brother and sister, I had my own bedroom, and by virtue of the "privacy" our bedrooms guaranteed, we were expected to experience a so-called full or rich inner life. We were permitted ———— even expected, though not required ———— to tape a "Private" sign on our respective bedroom doors. The life within was cavernous, unfathomable, deeply sedimented, and, even-tually, a prerequisite to naughtiness. I am like a house-painter, who cannot begin painting until the house is finished. And even that's not the entirety of the beginning. It has become obvious that some conflict has occurred or is about to. As the warming days of spring arrive, the trees wake up. With enormous effort, pushing and pulling, they draw the sap up into their highest branches and out into the tips of the twigs. And even before that task is done they have to push forth buds and then force them open. Flowers are the most violent of botanical beings ———— especially those that burst suddenly out of rent buds or split open the earth and erupt out of the soil. This is why girls love them. The element here that one could call <u>musical</u> is the never-quite contained totality, the changing topos. Now and then, intentionally, we strike a wrong note. I break six eggs into a large metal bowl and add some sugar. Success here depends on knowing both how much to wrestle with and how to wres-tle. The alternative is a failed happiness. "Night fell." No sentence could be simpler than that, few sentences could be more reassuring. Its past is a narrative past, bound to a temporal zone preserved for the past of things that are passing before us in the present whose future is what holds our interest: and then? Starting from the top, I sweep the steps in front of the house, moving the leaves, dust, scraps of paper, a dead beige furry moth missing a wing (if its wings had been intact I would have added it to the collection of insect specimens I have rescued from immediate obliteration and accumulated, each in a tiny plastic box on my desk), a bit of foil candy or gum wrapping, etc. —— all the debris that drifts onto the steps —— downward to the sidewalk. I scoop it into a dustpan and, with a commingled sense of remorse, sentiment, guilt, and mild anxiety, dump it into the garbage can. History can make even the happiest person terrible. Confronted by a situation that lacks fundamental credibility, one's anxiety increases, even as the ability to be interested in it dissipates. I have smashed the clock radio, shattering the microchip and breaking the minute copper and silver wires. Bits of pulverized electronics fall onto the table, but I sweep them up and, lifting the radio off its base, I drop them onto it and replace the radio on the base. Now the structure looks intact, though it can no longer register the passage of time nor communicate; my secret is safe. Sincerity, which might have been suspect, can now range more actively and articulate its own suspicions. A work of art is, in fact, a zone, the extent and activity of which produces an ongoing situation. For George Oppen, there is an epistemological valence to the notion of "sincerity": sincerity is requisite for a properly cognitive encounter with, and avowal of, the reality of things. Sincerity may seem to be the locus of immediacy for Oppen, but more properly it is the locus or even mode of curiosity. It would be ludicrous to imagine darkness as something voluntary. The Q in question is for the quizzical. "What can I do to help," I ask, and the woman at the stove says, "Everything." As an exercise in imagination, let's take the watercolor paints in Marcel Duchamp's lovely "Sonata" as the medium for the practical application of an emotion. In this case it is applied maternal satisfaction. In James Joyce's Dubliners, description might be the medium for the application of anger, and the bizarre projections that Charles Fourier sketched into his writings are a medium for the application of compassion. I'm always slightly pleased at my small outbursts of "athleticism" —— lightly running up a flight of stairs, gracefully climbing a fence —— and I willingly take up a wire whisk and begin beating the cream. I keep at it stubbornly until my arm aches, though it refuses to thicken. The block-long stretch of College Avenue between Russell Street and Ashby is lined with small, mundane neighborhood shops. As I walk by them, they seem ponderous; none of them are playful. I'll grant those on the west side of the street a place on a list: the ELMWOOD HEALTH AND MERCANTILE (previously the ELMWOOD PHARMACY, but Vicki the proprietor couldn't afford to keep on the dour pharmacist, and the whole place is within a few days now of going out of business altogether); MRS. DALLOWAY'S GARDEN AND LITERARY ARTS (a thriving independent bookstore on the premises of what, under a previous owner, was called Avenue Books); SHANGRI LA (a new shop selling Asian clothing and bric-a-brac); 14 KARATS (one of the neighborhood's enduring businesses, a jewelry store run by a portly, affable man and his wife, who used to work around the corner at the now defunct produce shop BURNAFORD'S); SHEN HUA (the first successful restaurant after a sequence of failures, including an Indian and then an Italian establishment); PAPYRUS (one of a chain of greeting card, wrapping paper, specialty invitation shops, with rapidly changing personnel); LORA'S CLOSET (a children's clothing shop, specializing in used clothes, wooden toys, and seconds); PANACHE (a hip hair salon); FILIPPO'S (a mediocre Italian restaurant); BLOOMING ALLEY (a flower stall situated in the alley connecting the west side of College Avenue to a small parking lot); LA MEDITERRANEE (an inexpensive, popular restaurant specializing in generic "Mediterranean" cuisine); YOUR BASIC BIRD (a pet store, its interior a cacophony of parrot calls, budgie squeaks, and fluttering canaries and finches); C & C CLEANERS (run by a Korean couple with a handsome young son and a tiny dog that always sits in the doorway); an empty shop (formerly JOHN'S, a shoe repair shop, and now under renovation); D-ZIRE (a hair salon); ICI (an ice cream shop offering "gourmet" flavors [honey lavender, green tea ice milk, rosemary dulce de leche, crème fraîche muscat] as well as vanilla and chocolate); LOLA (a gift shop); LULULEMON (purveyor of expensive athletic clothing and yoga classes). We are torn between contrary desires, on the one hand for repetition and recurrence (which we pursue by remembering) and on the other hand for novelty (for which we sample and browse). When does the insatiable desire for novelty emerge? Perhaps in the wake of Western secularization and the concomitant "age of exploration." The quest for knowledge couldn't be satisfied with familiar things; little as the nature of familiar grains, the everyday rising and setting of the sun, etc., has been understood, the quest for knowledge has remained primarily attracted to novelty, difference. Preference for quandary, queasiness, and quarrel is rare. In the early days of the Language Writing scene, it was not just structures and methods we changed; we also changed each other. And thus each of us over time has become less like the others. The changes occurred through interactivity, and the result was diversification, argument, improvement (let's hope), and also, of course, intensification. We revised, not through agreement and resemblance but through differentiation. We diverged, making more and more room for radical variations. It would be a mistake, however, to think of this as the triumph of individualism. A better analogy is to the "two hostile brothers" in the story of internecine warfare. When the phrase first comes up, one wonders what were they fighting over: a throne, a woman, an inheritance, property? But these two hostile brothers are not hostile to each other; they are comrades, a pair of hostile brothers, united in opposition to... to what we call the ineluctable display of thinking to oneself ———— the self-addressed inner monologue; it is always far from sincere. It's in the always ironic silence, in the sentimental aperture, that the real effects of sincerity writhe. The treetops, blown by the wind, boughs rising and falling, leaves fluttering and even flaring, their undersides flashing ———— the beauty of it all (and it is beautiful) is spontaneous and furtive, tentative, but continuous too, so that it seems also authoritative ———— though just what "it" refers to here is hard to identify: "it all?" Christa Wolf (in One Day a Year) defines "politics" as "distributing power." That might be accurate, at least up to a point, although only if we recognize that distributing power assumes the power to distribute and therefore must be preceded by the acquisition of power ——— which is another possible definition of "politics." An analogous definition of "capitalism" doesn't work, however: "capitalism" cannot be described as "distributing wealth." Far from it! That's precisely what capitalism doesn't do. What might once have been construed as a culture of distraction, hailing and hallucinating its citizenry, is now a domesticity of distraction, identical with subjectivity itself. We are the spoils, displaying ourselves in celebration of capitalism, like ghouls celebrating rotten flesh. In one story, a famous Polish linguist eats a bit of his third potato; wonderful, he calls it, the best, "though provincial." He claims that somewhere in northern Canada live the last two speakers of an indigenous language, but they have argued and are no longer on speaking terms. This is most likely an "urban myth," like the popular belief that hummingbirds migrate by riding on the backs of geese. In fact, hummingbirds migrate much farther and travel closer to the earth's surface than geese, which fly at 20,000 feet and higher. The sun hangs from a dangling filament torn from a web. Everything yields to the binding freedom generated by self-consciousness. For anyone interested in the unfolding of ideas, and in their subsequent displacement under the pressure of alternative ideas, and in the contingent materials that destabilize the contexts in which they are ideas about something, nothing can be entirely literal.

5

Sun, o sun, roaring day and night, is it you who sucks the wind into the trees at dawn as you rise. The sun is moving time, burning in the sky. With its gravitational pull it drags the past into its flames. But there's a countervailing force by which the light escapes. The past is cast into the present, which draws it in and then has to figure out what to do with it. Innumerable futures, all uncontained, each capable of reconfiguring the world, none fully imaginable, remain possible. Time can perhaps throw the future out. The blossoms are already falling from the plum trees along the edge of the parking lot, the petals, crushed by tires, are purpled and wet. I'm waiting for a sound, and it comes, almost immediately: a whistle, four notes of some melody. It's audible through a moment of relative silence between the cranking and crashing of the garbage collectors at work, whistled by one of them. To exist at a micro level, drawing and drawn to the bark of the plum tree and its shadow, thrown by the early morning light, and to metamorphic rocks and ant colonies and salt and a thistle and shingles and the complex social life of civic spaces and neighborhood interiors, and to do so freely, uncategorized, unidentified: this might be a description of an incipient condition ——— a beginning (a process of synthesizing). Or it might describe a late one. There's a vague, perhaps tragic, undertow, but its effects are less alarming than amusing ——— discomfiture, or embarrassment, or the pleasure brought on by a successful joke. "'What regiment is your son with?' a lady was asked. She replied: 'With the 42nd Murderers'." She has, Freud tells us, replaced the word Mörser (mortars) with Mörder (murderers). The resulting insight reveals more than this poor mother's guilty conscience. Freud's Psychopathology of Everyday Life is a book about bumbling, an unfolding comedy of errors, but it's often a tragicomedy: in its anecdotes, confessions, and analyses we can discern bits of a fragmented tragedy, awkwardly encountered by the book's diverse personae, or, as sometimes happens, the tragic scrap is just barely avoided, and one can't help but feel that further experience of it is merely getting deferred. "I entered a house and offered my right hand to my hostess. In a most curious way I contrived in doing so to undo the bow that held her loose morning-gown together." To horde knowledge would be to remove it from the flow of captions. A secret so secret that nobody knows there's a secret is an example of uncaptioned knowledge. Other secrets ——— all those whose substance remains unknown but whose existence is known ——— belong properly over the caption flow labeled, precisely, <u>Secret</u>. Ultimately, standards of respectability are irrelevant to the creative process. Leo X. Lee leans against the right fender of his old Toyota and absent-mindedly begins scratching a face into the worn burgundy paint with his car key. It follows the contours of a pock mark in the fender and the faded color around it. Russell Wright has the hood up and is trying to angle a wrench into place behind the radiator. Leo pockets the key. "You resent having to fix cars when you ought to be practicing?" "Machines. Music. You got to have different centers of gravity." Russell Wright gives a laugh. "Guess that's my woman problem, though." "What's going on with Rosa-Jane?" "I try to see her regularly. I feel sort of responsible." Russell Wright likes to play around with words, he likes suffixes. "Profligate, prolific, pro-ductive, professional ——— might be a lot of connections," he says. "Pro-vincial ——— that's what we're gonna be if we can't get gigs outside of Oakland," says Leo X. Lee. Russell Wright closes the hood and steps back. "Okay then." Leo drops Russell off at 49th Street and drives downtown to the Oakland MAP. The sun burns to excess. It is not simply causative, it produces (as Elizabeth Grosz says of <u>chance</u>) a "superfluity... of causes, the profusion of causes, which no longer produces singular or even complex effects but generates events, which have a tem-poral continuity quite separate from that of their 'causes.'" Along with forces of causation come forces of attraction. They pull and complicate. Love and hate, which seem so often prod-ucts of chance rather than intention, are really only false simplifiers (even as it is false to simplify them). Living under the sun requires receptivity and considerable frustration. A reader takes advantage of the light, but she cannot act on the knowledge she has so as to change what happens in the book she is reading; she is powerless to change the fate of its characters. This is the pathos of the reader. The sun draws life out. We lose an hour. Mounds of nasturtium sprawl over the edge of the sidewalk. Chance adds to the world's array of attractors, novelty rearranges the centers of gravity. The dialectical turbulence and flow in which intentionality and the unpredictable, plans of action and the inadvertent and contingent and unprecedented, displace one another are what keep the future open. Statewide protest rallies are planned for March 4: "March Forth on March Fourth" say the posters and flyers that students and union workers have been distributing. Just as quickly as they are pasted or pinned or taped or stapled to telephone poles and walls and bulletin boards and fences on the university campus, the campus police tear them down. Meanwhile, casual acts of passive resistance make use of anti-gravitational forces to make their case and effect their goal. "Not to notice the accoutrements of [...] power, not even to glance at the royal robes, not to bother to look at the king —— to glance away from these matters of state —— is to begin to undo their hold...." "I get that," Flip says. "But the Oakland MAP going to be marching forth, that be right." "Okay then." Leo X. Lee plays an A. "Let's have discord," he says. Leo X. Lee is nervous. "As usual," says QJ. Leo plays the A again. "Flip ——A flat." "Where?" "G string." Flip looks at the guitar neck and then plucks the note. "Okay —— Diego, B flat and Carlotta, you play a B. Flip, another A flat and sustain it this time. On 4." Leo jabs his right forefinger into the air and on the fourth beat the chord resounds. "Shit," says QJ. "Okay. Now stick to that one tone, but move it around —— play the pitch wherever you can find it on your instrument. Make it rock. And after a minute or so, QJ, you come in —— high hat only." "That chord is fuckin' meta," says Ravi Abedourian as he walks out of the room. The goal-oriented impulse in humans is destined never to be fulfilled. Or, rather, it is already fulfilled, but humans tend not to know this. As Nietzsche says, "[I]n the end there is no goal; we are always already at it. The fulfilled moment does not lie in the future, but is always there already.... Life does not follow the principle of linear accumulation and progressive enhancement, but instead revolves in a cycle of expiring and expanding.... For this reason, life is always already at its goal or remains equally remote from it, which ultimately amounts to one and the same thing." Yes, but one has to make this into more than vulgar fatalism's account of the human condition or stoicism's call to fortitude and fatalism. A pedestrian ———— a girl in a gray hoodie and short skirt ———— appears just one event (say a skateboarding boy leaps over a log, robs a bird's nest of an egg while still afloat over his board, hits the board again on his right foot, and kicks a cop in the balls with his left) prior to her turning into the alley that leads from the parking lot to College Avenue. Everyday life (more repetition) isn't a gap in the real, it's not a dead zone in the arena of power. Familiar narratives go largely unnoticed, something that people inhabit for varying lengths of time or that they pass through like circus clowns chasing each other into the tent, under the trapeze, and around the rings until they encounter the lions and bolt. The pull of something carnivalesque converges with the pull of commerce. In the process a glitch has arisen in the operating system along the western side of the street. A crowd blocks the way. The amblers, the lunchhour hospital technicians turning into CAFÉ ROMA, the neighborhood residents picking up cleaning from C & C, the people hurrying somewhere north or south with their eyes to the ground, the panhandlers (selling copies of the Quaker tabloid Street Spirit for $1 each or selling nothing but their own misery), are all more or less unconsciously aware of each other, all maintaining a modicum of safety and civility so that they can move along and not stumble or collide. But in front of ICI, whose interior is badly laid out and too small for the number of clients its expensive "hand-crafted" ice cream attracts, a crowd collects, forming a line that clogs the narrow sidewalk. Pedestrians are forced to step into the traffic-congested street, ducking around parked cars, and avoiding passing ones ———— a white PT Cruiser, a blue Honda Civic, several gray cars, a burgundy Prius, a red sports car ———— and a pick up truck, a brown UPS truck, an alternatingly sighing and grumbling city bus sounding as disgruntled as I (selfishly, or, worse, self-righteously) feel having to make my way through or around the crowd of people waiting for ice cream and completely indifferent to pedestrians' attempts to get by. Everyday life (culling repetition) swirls around absorptive narratives of no great interest whose importance and meaning and even genius are to be found in their for the most part trivial details. Saint Augustine regarded time as a theological perplexity; Shakespeare (and of course myriad other poets, humanists, feminists, physicists, and artists) considered it a problem for beauty and for the individual in relation to the pull of his or her ultimate mortality.

6

Despite confusing display, unyielding surfaces, the city is not inhospitable to a competent culinary shopper, an expert at gathering groceries. She is impervious to ploys, indifferent to novelty. There is no longer anything new, nothing new happens anymore. This is the conclusion toward which Nietzsche points with his aperçu that "God is dead." As Walter Benjamin points out, since then humans have had "to face with heroic composure" the eternal return of the same. But even that heroism is lost to us now. Everything is new and that is what's no longer new ———— the lack of novelty in the endless iterations of newness. Nothing old occurs anymore, either, except novelty's old news. History, in that sense, is dead too. Everything is the same. It is all hum and grid. Rhubarb is rote; edamame has entered Standard English. There are two large supermarkets equidistant from the building in which I live, one ten blocks south, one ten blocks northwest. I am entirely familiar with the way they are laid out. Produce to the right as one enters the door, against the wall. Citrus first. Nonetheless, shocks proliferate; what returns is perpetually unfamiliar ———— every commodity is unprecedented, though unsurprising. Within every story another story is hidden, autonomous and unfolding though scarcely noticed except now and then, inadvertently, when, just as with a slip of the tongue a woman exposes a bit of the turbulent life underway in her unconscious mind, a rat scurries through an open window with a doll's head in its mouth, or a man shouts a couplet from a passing bus:

> o queens of urbanity, kings of the crush
> let's sing of convenience, importance, and plush

Feral children come off the fire escapes. A highly educated mother masturbates triumphantly. Her name may be Alice Milligan Webster, but that name is significant only to those for whom it names her ———— it has only that local significance, if any. The city has 101,377 names, around 9800 per square mile. Maxine Able Smith, Leo X. Lee, Charles Altieri, Maggie Fornetti, etc. The sun emits a continuous roar, but from such a distance that it doesn't seem it can possibly be addressing any of us. With the death of the ahistorical or prehistorical God, history should have been born; sense perceptions should be able to discern something of the past, which bears the meanings and functions of the things that come before them. But history has no face. The shoppers flock to kiss the gleaming lemons. The city rumbles with unsubdued composure; its buildings betray little of what goes on inside them. The city players and planners all keep a low profile and work fast. They are left to their proliferating tasks. And, like Don Quixote, the literary scholar sets forth to do her work. Why like Quixote? Because what she engages with doesn't exist. There was no Emma Bovary to dream Madame Bovary's dreams. And if the literary scholar asks if the nameless narrator of Henry James's Turn of the Screw has really seen a ghost, the answer is that there was no nameless narrator but only the narration, with its ambiguous progress. Entering the supermarket with an empty cart pulled from the chain of carts standing ready by the door, I turn sharply to the right, past the avocadoes to the melons, in front of which I park my cart out of the flow of other shoppers. I move like an unregulated chess piece across the large checkerboard pattern formed by the floor's square tiles. Madame Bovary was Flaubert's "book about nothing," a test of "the axiom that there is no such thing as subject —— style in itself being an absolute manner of seeing things." Flaubert took on Guy de Maupassant as a student of sorts. "[Flaubert] forced me to describe, in a few phrases, a creature or an object so that it was clearly distinguishable from all other creatures or objects of the same race or species.... Homework consisted of a practical exercise: observe a grocer on his doorstep, a concierge smoking his pipe, or a cab-horse in a row of cabs, and then, 'with a single word,' show how that particular grocer, concierge, or cab-horse resembles no other." I tear off a plastic bag and reach over a display of parsley; I select a single head of butter lettuce from the dewy, vernal, green display. The tips of its outer, darker leaves are imperfect —— they are slightly torn and rust-stained, travel-worn. But the inner leaves are a pale, delicately variegated green, tender without being limp. This is the most succulent of lettuces. I've now added a cucumber, a head of endive, and a rubber-banded bunch of scallions to the shopping cart. I'm letting myself go. Long ago, <u>little</u> Lyn was in the produce section of a grocery store eating raw peas from the pod; <u>big</u> Lyn can remember the pods, the peas, the bin, the wood floor, the handsome, genial grocer: Roy of Roy's Market whom little Lyn carefully conflated with Roy Rogers, whom interim Lyns have had little occasion to remember, and whom big Lyn recognizes to have been carefully produced and like an animated porcelain (and later plastic) doll. A commodity. The radio cowboy offered an aberrant alternative to the possible ways and places one might live an everyday life (spectral repetition) ——— in an unfenced sprawl. Who offered him? To whom? Why? It's all a war zone but not to those who've imposed a deadline on abundance. Or it's all an ear exam testing for timbre-sensitivity rather than an ability to catch the drift of melodies. Everyday city life is a macrosystem, naturalized into invisibility, sometimes oppressive and sometimes so transparent as to seem to leave living unimpeded, nothing but green lights and a clear conscience and prospects or detritus: a black lacquer vase in an antique shop window; property lines; the drift of history; radiators; a small dish of potato chips; a photo of a dead man; reading glasses; Telegraph Avenue and Postcolonial Cul-de-Sac; the pungent smell of a tomato plant; a college education; a city-wide strike; anxiety: "[T]he true object of anxiety is precisely the (over)proximity of the Other's desire." Is the problem that the Other will impose his or her desire on one, that one will be forced to satisfy the Other's desire, rather than one's own, leaving one's own desires unsatisfied? Or is the problem that the Other's desire, when seen too closely, is repulsive (this is what Slavoj Žižek suggests, but it seems equally likely that, when forced to look too closely at one's own desire by the confrontation with the Other's, one will find one's own repulsive). I develop a few animosities as I gather groceries, and here and there a fleeting sense of camaraderie. There are countless ways to combine existences. Clearly there is much of myself that I want to present here. A novelist is in many ways like a ringmaster and a sociologist. He or she announces, and thereby calls, people into view, where they are fated to perform and to fare (poorly or well). An essayist is, however, a performer ———— an athletic bareback rider or juggler or high wire walker or trapeze artist, or one of the clowns: whapping or being whapped by other clowns, wig flying into the ether on a string, shoes flapping, pants dragging, jumping into a barrel over which a lion leaps while elephants trumpet and a monkey plays a drum. The clowns are variously criminals or detectives or victims of life or celebrants of the moment, giddily delinquent, or altogether earnest. The public pays to play its part, that of being the public. Willem is discerning, Bill is demanding, Betsy Warren is devouring, Rick Quincy is disdaining, and Askari Nate Martin is no longer detecting; he has long ago left Sue to be dismayed and Sid to stay away. The sunlights are multiple, refracting a city with a "Mediterranean feel" and hills. Boys and young women in uniform follow Sid, they go from one circus to the next. Dropping a baggie of sunflower seeds and a baggie of oats into her cart, and leaving it where it stands, Alice Milligan Webster backtracks a bit and goes down aisle 4 to get a jar of marmalade, which is among the jellies and jams just past the peanut butter and honey and across from the candy near the front of the store. She never drives her cart into the aisles and feels a twinge of approval as she overhears Austin White say to Betsy Warren, "You don't need the cart if you're just going halfway down the aisle for a box of sugar." Alice Milligan Webster is a person who accepts her fate and believes it is never the function of family life to subtract members; family life is all about addition and flow. Life is subject to "false halts" more than to "false starts." The revolutionary task before us is to create conditions in which the old and the new can occur again. History is to be resuscitated, though the disaster of monotheism should be avoided. With private ownership of land, myth-enchanted social culture along with its myth-suffused, story-bearing spaces came to an end. Monotheism is the religious principle closest to the sensibility of the home-owner. The heavens ceased to be social. Our identities are no longer bolstered, we have to reconfigure the world in such a way as to admit all that gives evidence of existing along with us. It is from kernels of impersonality ———— the fruits of the public sphere, where events and incidents that are not of one's doing, fragments of other people's existence, are encountered by chance ——— that one becomes a person in the city. I find myself watching a tall, shabbily-dressed man wheeling a grocery cart south along Seventh Street in which a fat woman in an overcoat is crouched, holding a paper bag. The rules that establish a relationship between them, and between them and me, and between me and the intrusive friendliness of the tellers at the bank I enter after noticing them, are derived from the game called "Napkin and Knife." As Peggotty remarks in David Copperfield, "I don't know how it is, unless it's on account of being stupid, but my head never can pick and choose its people. They come and they go, and they don't come and they don't go, just as they like." Everyday life (blatant repetition) is perpetually erupting into space and withdrawing from it. But to call it "erupting" suggests something abrupt. Public urban space, even the smallest, is analogous to a pause, however long prolonged, but it bears affinities with rest, too, and with patience, however sorely tested. Visitors may walk through it, residents may inhabit it, cars and buildings and pedestrians and noise may crowd it, and animals may traverse it or scuttle along its margins. It is available and accessible for cohabitation and communication, for acts of sharing, interacting, play, public displays of affection, flaunting, vying, acknowledging. People are out, strolling, hurrying, socializing, lining up, blocking the sidewalk, nodding to panhandlers, taking a break from their unshared and unshareable anxieties, fears, problems (or pleasures). Within the city's buildings, the immediate is under perpetual translation and transmission. To escape the barrage of media, we go out, away from our media-occupied private spaces (which the media renders strangely anonymous) and into public spaces: city streets, perpetually charged with anxiety and desire, and public parks, refuges for eccentricity and unproductivity. Everyday life (strange repetition) seeps from the city's interstices. I swipe the credit card and wait for the receipt to print out. The sun is coming through the doors. My arms straight, head up, pushing the bagged groceries in the cart in front of me, I make it to the car in nineteen strides.

Kiddies, kiddies, follow me
The streets, the trees, the feast, the sea.

It's a city with 36,485 actively managed street and park trees, which is to say <u>public</u> trees. They are unevenly distributed, abundant in the hills and more sparse in the more densely urban and industrial flatlands nearer the bay. The poor live on the hillsides above some cities (for example Rio de Janeiro and Mexico City) and the rich on the hillsides above some others (e.g., Berkeley and Oakland). It is among the labors of the poor to return home in the former and among the privileges of the rich to do so in the latter. Fragments of street music circulate ———— a bicyclist's bell, a siren, a vagrant with a guitar. Her beagle straining at the leash, a woman turns a corner and disappears. This isn't a city that "never sleeps." There's no bus service between 1 and 5 am. The city plot is knotted. It tangles conditions, situations, circumstances, terms which are not synonymous. The stronger the knots, the more vivid the plot. Dewanda Horn puts her body aside and, for an unperceived amount of time ———— it might have been hours, or only a few seconds, but it does not pass in increments, it is all of a piece, in a room, the windows open ———— she is but is not Dewanda Horn, sitting on a bench in the plaza with friends, facing away from the sun. Suddenly there's a tall hourglass-shaped cloud spinning toward us, blindingly white but dappled with dark markings, an hourglass cloud in the blaze of a rearing appaloosa. The massive twister grabs two women ———— I see them suspended upside down in the air, their dresses billowing. Then it's over, and we're standing in the plaza. Beside me is a young mother, holding a child; with her is Dewanda Horn. The young mother is weeping ———— she points to a photograph of herself with three children. "Two were taken away," Dewanda horn explains to me, "and they never came back." "And this one lost all her color," says the mother, looking down at her child, "and it never came back." I make a "to do" list ———— the happier version of the "did do" account that is the typical substance of a diary, in which, given the nature of the diary, there can no longer exist any reasonable hope. As morning returns, the sun recovers the city. Political struggle is not about ends but about beginnings. Political struggle seeks to open new possibilities for happiness ———— ordinary happiness, the happiness of ordinary lives. Thousands of peo- ple march through the city, chanting and brandishing signs and banners. They swarm through the streets approaching City Hall, they fill the Civic Center plaza with speeches and music. Protesting cuts to the budget for public education, protesting the emotional violence inflicted on poor people, students from Joaquin Miller Middle School are flying banners saying "Know All, Be All," "Don't Dumb Us Down," "Knowledge is Power," etc.

    So we appeal to you, sun, on this broad day.
    You were ever a helpmate in times of great churning,
    and fatigue.

7

Henri Lefebvre has said, "Everyday life is the supreme court where wisdom, knowledge, and power are brought to judgment." To the east of the airport a battalion of cattle is spread out over a hillside, briefly green and seeming almost even, unmarred, in what Charlotte Smith might have termed the perfecting light. Everyday life has palpable but abstract reality. It is sporadic but persistent, or, rather, it is continuous but unobtrusive. It's difficult to picture, it's a composite of contradictions, so dialectical as to be dizzying, though it is paradigmatically ordinary. Would that we could bring a term like polylectic to an account of this complicating operative condition but for now it is primarily applied to species of bees that collect pollen "from the flowers of a variety of unrelated plants." Everyone is going about his or her business. So are the spiders, and the molecules of asphalt, a tiny percentage of which get cast aside by passing automobiles every day. "Sounds penetrate partitions and wing their way through the walls of houses." This was true in Lucretius's time, as it is now. Everyday life (vernacular repetition) is everything that forms the common grounds, all that can be shared with other human beings, but some parts of everyday life ———— everyday indeed! ———— can't be shared with anyone. Wearing narrow-leg black jeans, a V-necked black sweater, and black socks, I go to CAFÉ ROMA for a double espresso and to read away from everyday life (laundry, dishes, email, egg-dying, sweeping repetition). Eventually I look up from a sentence ———— or part thereof ("The mouth that tells not will ever attract the unthinking tongue....") ———— startled by the intelligibility that thrusts it out of context (Finnegans Wake) and notice a small child looking around as he enters the café. He's wearing a knitted, black, hood-shaped hat along whose top, running from front to back, is an upright black and yellow crest of yarn. Wearing that hat, he sports a "Mohawk" rather than a mane, but either way he is a savage personage in a fantasy. With him are his grandparents ———— I know this because, as the trio passes me, I hear the woman refer to the man as "Grandpa": "Grandpa's going to buy us each a treat." Grandpa is a tall man with curly gray hair to his neck and a neatly trimmed beard. The grandmother is animated, perhaps anxious, and wearing a long beige wool coat and brown scarf. They sit directly behind me. "I have a secret friend," the little boy says; he's no more than four years old. "You do?" says the grandmother, eagerly. "Tell me about him ———— or is it a girl? Is it a boy or a girl?" "A boy!" "Tell me about him," she offers. "Never!" Not everything that invites interpretation is allegorical. Indeed, not everything invites interpretation. But much does, or so human beings feel. Established practices and personal habits ripple through everyday life, but so, too, do ritualistic behavior and magical thinking. Moment-to-moment choices and decisions are as apt to be governed by idiosyncratic superstition as by sense or assessment. Whenever a recipe calls for garlic, I add an extra clove or two, for protection of life and limb. I sit toward the left in a movie theater, so as to occupy, literally, a leftist position. But here superstitious behavior is a joke. What might an avant-garde look like now ———— as an aesthetic practice and/or as a social practice? It begins as an oppositional practice, but if it remains only that, or principally that, it dooms itself to continuing dependence on the very thing it opposes. And, since currently "the very thing it opposes" is likely to be the conditions of late capitalism, the next question to ask is, how does an artist produce anything that could be properly called "avant-garde" when relentless (capitalist) innovation and shock are precisely the problem at hand? Fredric Jameson offers one tentative answer, though in the context in which he does so, he is talking about the discourse of theory rather than the arts of the avant-garde. "There... emerges a... possibility: namely, what I will call the production of theoretical discourse par excellence.... This activity is utterly nontraditional and demands the invention of new skills altogether. New theoretical discourse is produced by the setting into active equivalence [which is not to be confused with "identity"] of two [but I don't see why there couldn't be more than two] preexisting codes.... What must be understood is that the [resulting] new code (or metacode) can in no way be considered a synthesis between the previous pair [or set].” Jameson imagines this in terms of <u>two</u> preexisting codes, because he is concerned with dialectical processes, however novel their configuration and unpredictable their outcome. But this new “possibility” is more complicated ——— and perhaps more fulfilling ——— than classical dialectics, since the whole undertaking may serve an unresolving function. If and when the two or more codes are mutually contradictory or incommensurate with each other, what may result are, as Jameson points out, “strange new ambivalent abstractions” ——— but I don’t know why they can’t equally well be strange new ambivalent <u>concretions.</u> One doesn’t mop the kitchen floor out of conviction, nor to fulfill a fantasy, but nonetheless doing so is part of a commitment to a social aesthetics that is deemed critical. Mopping is an avowal of the value of something. The term “avant-garde” has fallen into the scrap bin of history and has been supplanted in the last thirty or more years by such unimpressive terms as “experimental” and “innovative.” As modestly descriptive or weakly categorical labels, these may still be useful ——— but they say little and tend to serve careerist rather than expansive, inventive, or semantically radical purposes. Furthermore, they are most often applied not to socio-cultural or aesthetic tendencies but to literary and artistic <u>styles</u>, many of which exist precisely so as to situate the work within the (marketable) sphere of the experimental and/or innovative. Fragmentation, syntactic deformation, non-linearity, lexical invention, collage, ambiguity, etc. ——— such devices are no more <u>definitive</u> of avant-garde work than of <u>The Canterbury Tales</u> or <u>The Life and Opinions of Tristram Shandy</u>. Wearing a hoodie is not a manifestation of criminal intent; it can’t even make one cool or young, not to mention male or black. Shifting slightly in my chair in Café Roma, I turn to look again at the little boy in the crested hat. I was wrong to see the crest as resembling a “Mohawk” hairdo. The hood-like hat isn’t a wig, it’s a helmet. The child is a warrior, a knight. On the left side of the hat, woven into the fabric from the top of the boy’s ear to the edge of his chin, is an image of a human skull. Before a bird catches the boy’s attention and he turns to look back at the open doorway, I have a side view of his head and of the skull inside it. The child, as a knight, carries on his head a <u>memento</u>

mori. A house sparrow has hopped into the café through the wide doorway. From the ground it sings, over and over, "Don't dumb it down to me." The effect is beautiful. A metaphor is a unit of proffered interpretation; an allegory invites one to interpret for oneself. All important modern art reflects strife, undertakes resistance. This has been true for over a century, and one could argue that this is because the period itself has been one of unprecedented strife, marked by wars (declared and undeclared, hot and cold) but also, and more pervasively, by capitalism, which is itself an economics, and hence a social politics, of strife. Capitalism, to succeed, increasingly provokes frenzy, not tranquility. "Modernism dreamed of aesthetic universals that could provide civilization with culture," Charlie Altieri says. "Postmodernism found itself in a world of multiple cultures and discovered that universals are impossible." I am not against interpretation. On the contrary, it is an activity I tend to engage in with near abandon, seduced by the cognitive pleasures and constructive possibilities it promises, though usually, at interpretation's end, I'm aware of the arbitrariness, or incompleteness, or gratuitous weirdness, or obviousness, or heavy-handedness of its outcome. Inevitably, interpretation falls victim to the interpreter's limiting motives and motivations. Every metaphor, too, imposes limits. As a paradigmatic interpretive medium, it can be problematic in several ways. First, it can be prejudicial, deformative as much as it is informative. This was the basis for Sir Francis Bacon's objection to any use of metaphor in descriptions of natural phenomena; scientific inquiry should be addressed to raw data; new discoveries and thus new knowledge can't be based on data that's been familiarized or domesticated through comparison with things already known. Second, metaphors, properly speaking, offer a completed interpretation ——— a summation. With the appearance of the metaphor, the job is done. This is why extended metaphors are so often parodic rather than apt, comically excessive rather than assiduous. A possible third problem with the metaphoric is that it may offer an interpretation at the expense of the interpreted reality itself. In such a case, data hasn't merely been tampered with, it's been tossed aside altogether. Metaphors are units of understanding, not units of reality

———— though, undeniably, they carry bits of reality with them. Pan, with his florid or fiery face (it makes a difference which), is an allegorical image of the entire universe (<u>pan</u>), as a guy whose head is a sun. Or is it merely reflecting the sun? The ordinary, the quotidian, reality's scattered happenstantial trivia and people's repetitious personalia ———— it all passes under the sun. The sun: productive and purposeless and not always benign, all-powerful and essential and definitively <u>everyday</u>. In <u>The Psychopathology of Everyday Life</u>, among the many anecdotes that Freud tells as a joke on himself, is this one, which may be more self-revealing than Freud realized: "For some time I used to carry a stick with a silver handle. On one occasion the thin metal got damaged, through no fault of mine, and was badly repaired. Soon after the stick came back, I used the handle in a mischievous attempt to catch one of my children by the leg ———— with the natural result that it broke, and I was thus rid of it." Is it the stick or the kid or the leg of the kid that Freud wants to rid himself of. The scenario's plot is harbored by its syntax, maintained by the ambiguity of pronouns. But this is apt, since, as Henri Lefebvre notes early in the first volume of <u>The Critique of Everyday Life</u>, "ambiguity is a category of everyday life, and perhaps an essential category." The wide broadcloth shades are pulled down over the high windows of the lecture hall, but a soft gray band of late afternoon light slowly forms on the floor near the podium. An hour goes by. Overhead the sun captions the moon, arched like a herring in the pale day sky, and a fictional character I'll call Nicholas Declan Callahan is walking down the steps in front of the neo-classical public building, headed with Sammy Christine Blake toward a café across from the plaza. "History reads the past as the prehistory of the present ———— that's kind of exactly what Peter Bürger says ———— and that's only half the story," says Nicholas Declan Callahan, who likes to continue, so he goes on: "I think we could look into the past to see what we're missing." "That's the fast track to nostalgia," says Sammy Christine Blake. "I don't mean corsets and claret and Oliver Twist," says Nicholas. "I mean the future ———— what we can't see in the present and don't expect." "You'd have to cancel the present for that," says Sammy, brushing her right hand across the tattoo on her left shoulder, "which could be a good thing, but you'd still be looking from the present's per-spective." A little way south of the plaza pedestrians are moving past a stretch of neighborhood shops. By the bank a fat pan-handler sits, doleful, aggressive, and indomitable. In front of the ice cream boutique, clumps of socializing shoppers block the sidewalk. A woman ——— a neighborhood regular ——— has-tens by, stepping off the curb to get around them. She irritably recognizes herself as just one of many competing presences, reciprocally anonymous, equally entitled to the sidewalk, and takes the shortcut through the short alley between FILIPPO'S and LA MEDITERRANEE. In what language-game do we com-bine the terms time and being into a single term ——— as in "the time being"? I can't think of the phrase as occurring in anything but the prepositional phrase "for the time being." Why that particular preposition? And why do we speak of the time being but not a time being? Is there no indefinite time being? At some level, explicit or, more likely, implicit, a work of art confronts the question of "how to live the good life." The sun-light fades and the blue of the sky, the sky bluing all day ——— cobalt, or turquoise, then eggshell blue ——— disap-pears. Over a dark residential street in the neighborhood, Venus is visible. The way Maggie Fornetti knows about things is by adding to them. The same is true for Askari Nate Martin, but awareness that possibilities are infinite doesn't thrill Askari Nate Martin nor excite his curiosity; it makes him nervous, wary. It is the secret to his autonomous mien and the reason he is no lon-ger a police detective. "You've seen the 'What I Do' column?" Askari Nate Martin nods but says nothing to the interviewer, Rosa-Jane Stein. "It's just fluff ——— human interest shit, that humans don't find interesting." Nate nods again, his slight smile quizzical, asymmetric. "Thanks for agreeing to be interviewed," says Rosa-Jane Stein. "No problem," Askari Nate Martin says. Rosa-Jane Stein sets the "voice memo" on her iPhone to record and asks him what he does. He doesn't want to call himself a director, doesn't want to claim that anyone can be said to "run" the Oakland MAP, so he says he works there. "Oakland MAP ——— the Oakland Music and Arts Program." "For kids," she says. "For kids." She wants to know what kind of kids, he avoids the terms "at risk," he calls them "talented." Some of them get recommended by their schools, a few come from an arts–oriented charter school and get credit for taking a semester–long class, a few are in the juvenile justice system, none of which he says. "Talented," he says. "I couldn't categorize them beyond that." It's misleading to associate the allegorical with metaphor; the allegorical is not analogic but indexical. It's syntactic rather than semantic, connective rather than comparativist. It's temporal as much as it's spatial. It is tempting to call it narrative rather than representational, but it's more accurate to regard it as a representation of narrativity, an affirmation of the fact that everything exists within stories ———— that is, within, while also as, context. Say I want to concoct a tale based on the familiar objects in an ordinary room, a tale that would entertain a child without frightening him or her. "The bed is made of magic straw and the window panes of ice," I begin. But, unable immediately to imagine what magical properties might be appropriate to straw apart from its perhaps undesirable ability to turn into gold, I begin again. "The bed is an aeronautical vehicle, and the window panes are made of moonlight." It's better to call the bed an aeronautical vehicle rather than a flying bed, as the prospect of settling down to sleep in a bed that might fly could be terrifying for the child. On June 15, 1880, aboard a ship moving slowly through ice fields in the far north, the young Arthur Conan Doyle in his diary calls the wind "depraved"; six weeks later, he calls the fog "pusillanimous." Interpretations, including those skirted by digressions as well as those embodied in metaphors and reproduced by them, require comparisons. And those comparisons are made by humans, which should render them suspect much of the time, or, at the very least, themselves in need of interpretation. As Ernesto Grassi is compelled to note, though he himself is an advocate of metaphorical thinking, "The metaphor is… the originary form of the interpretive act itself, which raises itself from the particulars to the general through representation in an image, but, of course, always with regard to its importance for humans." With the words "happily ever after," a tale announces both the quality and quantity of its continuation. It accepts, gladly, the state of things now and anticipated and it has no discernable end; it is indeterminate in quantity and expresses minimal qualifications regarding the possibilities of a near painless life. Here, somewhat ineffectu-ally, like a woman in an audience shouting at the stage, I intercede: In her poem "The Labors of Hercules," Marianne Moore says, "one detects creative power by its capacity to con-quer one's detachment."

.

8

Swiftly and long of life is the cocked gaze of surveillance glowing in the corner of a student's future. The student stops, circles back, and photographs. Beside her, her friend the braggart sings:

> See he who glares with feral time eyes!
> See she who drops her spit on spies!

The braggart ———— I'll call him Victorion Inca Shushek ———— brandishes a blank placard. An old writer is happening by. "That's not art, baby, that's life," says Julian Earl French, moving carefully and leaning on his cane as he pauses to consider the placard. The old writer has lost interest in depicting his own particular perceptions of the world and aspires instead to depict the world as it is. But realities are at war. Or realities are proxies in a war ———— or many wars ———— abstractly waged, ambient, unnamed. Say a body has a left foot oddly placed, a right foot in its way, and is capable briefly of flight. What is Symbolism if not, as Arthur Symons put it, "that perfecting of form in its capacity for allusion and suggestion, that confidence in the eternal correspondences between the visible and the invisible universe"? Victorion Inca Shushek's placard requires a caption. Bodies require actions. We can generate a long list of requirements. Safety, for example. That should take priority over aesthetic interest, say, or novelty, or possibilities for interspecies communication. Context is another word for the vortices of causation. "You are making an ambiguous protest," says Julian Earl French to Victorian Inca Shushek. Vivid urban birds flutter around them, some launching into awkward flight, some just now returning to the plaza. They shimmer and shit. They eye reality, but ———— speaking for myself only here ———— I have to admit that I have no idea what reality they see. Probably not our beautiful, certainly not our political. They eagerly gather around a crust. "Did you ever think how much multi-paned windows look like a cage?" Jillie Jane Rogers gestures with her camera; Victorion Inca Shushek acknowledges the similarity with one quick nod. The aesthetic avant-garde searches for difference, even while the political avant-garde seeks similarity ——— common grounds, bases for critique, foundations for solidarity. The everyday life (unquiet repetition) we could call the "urban social" sustains clay, salamanders, chairs, milkweed, dog shit, ears, poplars, cabbage, and parking lots. Also rats, plastic bags, asphalt, jurors, rose bushes, Chihuahuas, pedestrians, and donuts. There is a very real paradox inhabiting everyday life, which is a reality, and has a realism to go with it, but, despite the innumerable beings, gestures, matters, materials, motives, norms, acts, and habits at play in it, and despite its ubiquity, we can't definitively and elementally picture it. This is just as well. Without any commanding image we await the utopian future, the happier world that we can't picture because we don't know what it would look like, and that we shouldn't picture because, if we do, it will be co-opted, commodified, and sacrificed in the arena of the spectacle. We know, of course, that there is a realm of materiality that belongs precisely to the orders of what does exist but isn't seen. This is partially the terrain of science ——— microbiology, quantum physics, etc. And it is partially the realm of the ubiquitous commonplace differential quotidian, which exists in the form of protracted processes and evolving situations that are lived over time. Friendship or domesticity or the unfolding history of a public plaza may produce patterns, but they aren't achieved in a moment. They occur in imperceptible increments, day by day, and, though they can be evaluated aesthetically, they can't be represented best or solely by the aesthetic. "How, then, can the aesthetic, which is incommensurable even for portrayal in poetry, be represented? Answer: by being lived." Or, as the art historian Michael Fried remarks in response to this aphorism of Kierkegaard's, everyday life "absolutely defeats being represented in and by the various arts, all of which fail in different ways to do justice to the sheer protractedness or extensiveness of time, but [...] it can be represented 'by living it, realizing it in the life of actuality,' in short by making existence itself an aesthetic medium." Victorion Inca Shushek is trying to crash through to that unpictured materiality. "I think it's allegorical," says Livia Columba Rock, looking at his sign.

And I agree. As Henri Lefebvre notes, "symbolism and praxis cannot be separated." We can caption what we can't see.

- The desirable maintains aesthetic distance
- The pigeon qua private eye
- Fear is an inconstant sadness
- The heroic spectator is overcome by obligations
- Don't blame your <u>eyes</u> for your world view

If you are reading this, then this is what you are doing here. Wherever the allegorical appears, there is sure to be a problem, generally a problem involving the translation, the transmutation, the transitoriness of ideas. Alan Hanif Alvarez crosses the street. A cluster of plaza police are standing near a kiosk under an urban tree. Too often, no doubt, the allegorical anthropomorphizes. Maintaining conceptual distance (as we can't help but do, given the limits of our experience and our susceptibility to fear), we might describe the ubiquitous igneous urban pigeon as a wary bird, catching neon, reflecting the viridian flash of the cobalt sky, suspicious, beady-eyed, scavenger-minded, constantly on the watch for whatever is to its advantage: grabbing a crumb, dodging a truck, securing a perch from which to shit and preen and coo. The pigeon taunts bankers qua bankers, bankers qua barbecuers, bankers qua boozers, qua bicyclists, qua bargain-hunters. At a small market across from the plaza a banker buys a half-pint of blueberries for $2.99, a turkey sandwich for $6.25, and a bag of pistachio nuts for $4.19. He pays in cash and receives his change in the palm of his mottled pink hand. Irregular white and gray-green blotches on the pavement are splattered at the edge of the intersection onto which a telephone pole casts a shadow. I stand in the shadow, out of the sun. <u>Point everywhere, demand nothing</u>. Lucretius says that "whatever exists must be something in its own right; and if it is susceptible of even the lightest and faintest touch, its very existence ensures that it will increase the aggregate of matter by an amount either great or small and augment the total sum." <u>The counter to fear, comrades, is camaraderie</u>. Let's take pleasure for a moment in the flutter of emotions that the taunting of bankers has stirred. There will be time enough later for prolonged embarrassment, lasting repercussions, and eventual retreat in victory, regret, or even in fear, that condition of unmitigated interiority, abyssal subjectivity. A flock of birds circles the plaza, two small dogs are chasing a squirrel around a tree, the protestors are chanting. Contexts are unfolding that even a movie couldn't represent. We live amidst and, however unconsciously, partake in constellations of the real that cultural standards, narrative givens, etc. can't make sense of, or even perceive. Simply to realize they are here, emitting flickers from the feathery increments of their iridescent half-lives, requires the kinds of time that we are rarely, if ever, permitted to have.

9

Everyday life subsides into insignificance even while we attend to it constantly. This is a paradox that perpetually complicates the quotidian milieu. It is ubiquitous, persistent, trivial, scattered unevenly across every duration, and difficult to think. Ubiquity, persistence, triviality, unevenness ———— these terms apply equally to everyday life (incidental repetition) and to the paradox. So too do vast, furtive, fleeting, serial. "I see the moon and the moon sees me and the moon sees somebody I want to see." In the bright afternoon sunlight, no moon is visible. Hannah Ming Hoover is singing to her fretful baby, seated on a low wall at the edge of the city plaza. The lyric "you" is preoccupied as it occupies the space in which the lyric "I" situates her imagined desires. For Hannah Ming Hoover, her fretful baby both is and isn't the lyric "you" of the moment. People in the plaza are interacting, often unconsciously, stories are unfolding, often with no remarkable significance to each other, motifs are in the air, people are talking about economic inequity, a dry winter, the "altruism gene," canine cops. People are exercising their intellectual freedom, though the exact sequence of words in which they express their ideas may end up typed into someone else's possession. Extended between two upper windows of the Multicultural Center hangs a banner: DECOLONIZE THE UNIVERSITY! ESPOUSE THE MULTIVERSITY! John Berger notes, in a passage affectionately addressed to Arundhati Roy, that political protest is undertaken not only, nor perhaps even primarily, on behalf of a better future but on behalf of the present moment. "One protests," he says, "in order to save the present moment, whatever the future holds." One does it because it is the good, the right, and even the happy thing to do ———— in that sense, okay, one does it for one's own sake. But more to the point, one does it for the sake of the moment. The protest makes the moment; it takes it on, realizes it. Everyone who participates will have participated in it. As the minutes go by, the sunlight varies in intensity, the shadows of cars parked on the street move even when the cars haven't. But their reach isn't infinite. In <u>Either/Or</u>, Kierkegaard's judgmental but not unkindly nor injudicious Judge William admonishes a hedonistic young man for whom he has great concern. "You want to satisfy the hunger of your doubt by consuming existence," he says to him. The young man is acquisitive (a seducer) but not possessive; like Shahryar (until he's educated by Scheherazade's thousand-night curriculum of nocturnal tales), the young man casts aside those he seduces once the seduction succeeds. The judge's remonstrance continues: "You readily admit that you are good for nothing, that your only diversion is to march around existence seven times, blow the trumpet, and then let the whole thing collapse so that your soul can be soothed, indeed, become sad, so that you can call forth echo, for echo sounds only in emptiness." It's on the forms —————the shapes —————of this negative space that I'm concentrating as Maggie Fornetti runs her finger back and forth over the handle of the cup in front of her, listening to Dewanda Horn, about to say something, a way of bestowing attention on the point Dewanda is making and the way she progresses toward that point. "You're leaving something out," says Maggie Fornetti. Invisibly, negative space provides structure. It's not just the lines in the space but also the spaces around and between the lines that construct the things around us —————rocks of a wall, children in a playground, a bicycle wheel, a tree at the edge of a city plaza. But it's impossible for images appropriate to the future yet to appear. Outside the café, under occasional clouds, three solicitors and one panhandler are working the block. Two of the solicitors are trying to raise money for the American Civil Liberties Union, the other for Greenpeace. The panhandler is working on his own behalf. I give him a dollar, playing my part in a social fantasy that insists on the shared nature of public space despite our experiencing the street very differently, and make a pretense of camaraderie which, if tested, would disappear, awkwardly and perhaps dangerously. Inside the café (CAFÉ ROMA, on the southwest corner of College Avenue, diagonally across the intersection from a WELLS FARGO BANK) are a heavy woman in a long purple cardigan (slice of cake and a cup of coffee), a florid man reading a magazine (bowl of chili and a glass of mineral water), a skinny close–shaven young white man reading a hardcover book (iced latte), two black men in track suits playing chess (a cup of coffee, a glass of milk), a white man in khaki shorts, blue t-shirt, and denim jacket accompanying an Asian woman, carrying a large canvas shoulder bag, and two children, a girl around eight and a boy around six (a cookie and small Italian soda for each of the children, a cappuccino for each of the adults), Maggie Fornetti and Dewanda Horn (cappuccinos), and Tamarind Magee with Lei–lei Wilson Tin and Lily Ball (sharing one Caesar salad and the slab of focaccia that comes with it). Rachmaninoff's 2nd Piano Concerto at low volume is coming through speakers set in two corners against the ceiling of the café. Writing about Pierre Bonnard's luminous late interiors, Rita Burnham makes this observation: "If he indeed conceived of consciousness itself as a fundamental tranquility that is ruptured by feelings and memories, this would in some sense account for many of the phantoms in Bonnard's work: the figures, the layered memories, that enter in at the edges of consciousness and sight, in moments of heightened awareness when feeling and memory are inseparable. Sometimes they materialize slowly; at other times they enter silently, spectrally, into the room. It often takes the viewer a very long time to see them." The process of doing so draws the viewer into what one might term the arduous aesthetic pleasure of remembering. The occasional figures within Bonnard's interiors, meanwhile, withhold narration. Or perhaps the narrative has been withdrawn from the scene. This lack of narrative might be the source of the tranquil consciousness that Burnham discerns (and which is probably not identical with Bonnard's own, which seems more disturbed than tranquil). The figures ——— or the parts of figures, the side of a face, a shoulder and arm, someone almost out the door ———are often visible only peripherally, at the margins of the room or merging with the furnishings and objects in it. They can only be glimpsed (they elude scrutiny), but one feels them. They are palpable more as sensation than substance. And they are as indifferent to us as the tabletops that figure so prominently in the paintings. The people who made the tables are more than invisible; they are altogether effaced from the time of the tables, or of the paintings, or of our looking at the paintings. But everyday life (enclave of repetition) is never anachronistic, never timeless. However intimately we are imbricated in its manifold elements, we are living historically ——— in the flow of social and economic exchange, in the transmission of power. "Beauty demands the present and is tormented because of that." Maggie Fornetti is, not un-self-consciously, at this moment paying close attention to Dewanda Horn, to what she is saying, and to the moment in which she is saying it. The sun is expanding the neighborhood through which vehicles, pedestrians, pets, children, residents, bugs, birds, visitors, bacteria, move in their efforts at perfection. At night the dark expands the neighborhood, too. These are two modalities of expansion, then, both finite, though in both space is added. "At times I feel that I am waiting for something that, when it occurs, I won't experience," says Dewanda Horn. There can be no meaningless imagined situation; no matter how bizarre, as imagined the situation has meaning. But the site of that meaning ——— its psychic location ——— may be so individual ——— so unique, singular ——— as to preclude that meaning's being set at large. The imagined situation is radically localized and perfectly limited, bound to and harbored in the psyche of he or she who imagines it, though linked to that of those with whom the situation is, even if only peripherally, shared. Maxine Able Smith considers her "everyday tasks" ——— feeding the cat, folding laundry, paying bills, shopping for groceries, cleaning the bathtub, responding to email ——— as being of such pressing and relentless importance that they often charge her with anxiety and a sense of self-righteousness. She has no alternative but to hurry. And yet she knows these tasks are trivial, everything could wait, the cat won't starve, the details of her life, in their near inconsequentiality and triviality and even banality, are both stupid and not quite identical to those of people living around her. She feels alien, she feels that her self-worth has no value here. "Meaningful only to me" is the way she regards her tasks as she addresses a birthday card to a distant cousin and feels a quickening of anxiety, needing to get the card in the mail immediately, while the laundry needs to get moved from washer to dryer, the potted plants on the porch need water, she's out of butter. "Meaningful only to me always needing something from me." She states this not apologetically but angrily and only to herself, the only one who cares, the only one worth reprimanding, the only one taking care of the tasks. If she had the nerve she'd tell other people just to fuck off, but she's a nice person: being nice is one of her tasks. She is busying herself with it as I write this. It's not justice if it's meted out, she thinks; meting is always stingy. This purely imaginary scene ———— concocted just now, I don't know how or why, by me ———— presumably means something to me. It may affect me. I'm accustomed to the panic of importance that everyday life (vertical repetition) can inflict. But, except insofar as I act in response to it, or carry out my normal ways of being in the world in terms of a psyche that can imagine such a (melancholy but also innocuous and ridiculous and strangely isolated) scenario, it has no effect on, or meaning for, the rest of world (defined as all that is not me). In all practical terms, I, in my imaginative act, become unreal. Ideas come to one intimately, even those that are meant for broad application, general acknowledgement, those that are expressed aphoristically, those that are conditioned by self-reflexivity. But dreams are far more impersonal than the fictions one concocts. I'm on an unmade bed. Suddenly the pillow moves. It quivers, pauses, then leaps. I understand: the material it's made of has the same properties as popcorn; under some excitative force, it's expanding. It takes off. It requires a response. We have an intellectual task to perform. The task is described; it comes in the form of a challenge, an announcement of what's at stake. There's an "immediate need for repossession! There are real concerns here!" The pillow that's become a man sags and falls silent; no one responds, everyone waits for it to continue. This is all image, with no future. "Even the lowliest of individuals has a double existence. He, too, has a history, and this is not simply a product of his own free acts. The interior deed, on the other hand, belongs to him and will belong to him forever; history or world history cannot take it from him; it follows him, either to his joy or to his despair." Here I stop to remind you, dear reader, that I am a woman. So where is my phallus? Don't look between my legs, dear. The phallus that was mine got free and now it's floating around on its own somewhere. In a room at the Oakland

MAP, Sophie-Ann Solander lifts a rung-backed chair onto a table and tells the kids to "draw everything that isn't the chair."

10

"The madman does not notice that he is changing subjects. He grasps a piece of shining yellow straw and shouts that he is holding the sun." Denis Diderot makes this observation to his beloved Sophie Volland in a letter dated October 20, 1760. That was more than 250 years ago. If anything were to last forever it would have to exist in a universe entirely invulnerable to temporal blows. I can hear the sound of the wind sweeping across the walls of the building, a distant dispiriting helicopter, a sequence of unpromising phrases running through my mind. I label myself discouraged, ebullient, angry, satisfied ——— or perhaps dissatisfied; I'm defiant, excited, tired, eager to understand (or, more likely, eager to unburden myself of) my feelings. The self-involvement of intellectuals of my social background is its own kind of madness. I tell myself I only have the machine, I'll only halve the machine, I've only half the machine. Ham hock heat wave, rosy dog-shit weed-lot daffodil, carousel broomstick broccoli-belt cyclist, low-tide mint-condition milkshake, mushroom-padded cardboard door, and honey bags. Everyday life (freestanding repetition) is going on pretty much as usual. But there are vagaries of context and sometimes turmoil, even sometimes states of perpetual upheaval. It's not only art that can intensify everyday life. In my opinion, we are currently living under siege, but the situation is so pervasive that it has come to feel natural, as do the forces by which we are besieged. Nonetheless, their pressure is increasing. We can apply an allegorical supplement to the situation. It can appear in the form of a caption ———whether or not it is visibly present as an inscription, as a title, legend, heading, name, or as an interpretive or critical thought, a mental addendum. We want it to point to a way out of the situation. The beholder declares to herself or to her companion, O, it isn't just a poem about a girl petting a swan, it's an ode to innocence as an unimpeded acceptance of meaning. Relevance means nothing; everything is suited to fantasy. It's all totally real. She feels it, the flow from swim to swan.

A good reader will, in time, open a poem to de-allegorization: O, she will say, this isn't an allegory, after all, it's a poem about a girl running her fingers down the surprisingly warm ———— almost hot ———— and thorny soft breast feathers of a real swan. The good reader continues, distributing (and sometimes dispensing with) her intentions. Still, she admits, even a thinly cut slice of rye bread on a little plate might be a clue to domestic confusion. Literary language can't escape reality, it's vivaciously additive, and it is with an addition of language that an object, image, or situation becomes allegorical and also still real. Something's common designation, its name ————Lyn Hejinian, Wheeler Hall, Paris ———— is rarely allegorical, and alternative names (nicknames: e.g., Lynnie; descriptives: e.g., the English Department building on the campus of the University of California, Berkeley; evaluative anaphoras: e.g., the greatest city of Europe) are not necessarily so, though the latter tend toward interpretive and captioning functions, which have strong allegorizing potential and sometimes exercise it. In 2008 a new edition of Merriam-Webster's Dictionary was published, with the inclusion of more than 100 new entries. Among them were air quotes: "gesture made by raising and flexing the index and middle fingers of both hands, used to call attention to a spoken word or expression"; edamame: "immature green soybeans, usually in the pod"; mental health day: "day that an employee takes off from work to relieve stress or renew vitality"; netroots: grassroots political activists who communicate via the Internet, especially through blogs; racino: "racetrack at which slot machines are available for gamblers." The 2010 OED added cat-astrophizing: "view or present a situation as considerably worse than it actually is"; overthink: "think about (something) too much or for too long"; matchy-matchy: "excessively color coordinated"; LBD: "little black dress"; frenemy: "a person with whom one is friendly despite a fundamental dislike or rivalry"; cool hunter: "a person whose job it is to make observations or predictions about new styles and trends"; bromance: "a close but nonsexual relationship between two men"; exit strategy: "a preplanned means of extricating oneself from a situation"; defriend: "another term for unfriend (remove someone from a list of friends or contacts on a social networking site)"; soft skills: "personal attributes that enable someone to interact effectively and harmoniously with other people." WWW. learn-english-today.com/new-words/new-words-in-english2. html includes in its lengthy list earworm: "a tune that keeps repeating itself over and over again in our heads"; foodoir: "a blend of 'food' and 'memoir,' an account of someone's life or personal experiences, with a strong emphasis on food, often including recipes and cookery advice"; gastrosexuals: "a new generation of men who see cooking more as a hobby than a household chore, and use their cooking skills to impress friends and potential partners"; meh: "interjection used to express indifference or to show that one simply does not care; equivalent to shrugging one's shoulders; used as an adjective it means 'mediocre'"; noughties: "the years between 2000 and 2009 which contain a 'nought' (zero), in the same way as other decades are called the 'thirties', 'sixties', etc." Contextualization is a process, an elaboration of conditions and circumstances, a flow of contingencies and interruptions (not of interpretations). Context is not so much definitive or determinative as prospective; many possible actualizations could take form in it. To the extent that we know it, it has informative but not necessarily explanatory potential. What's happening now can't predict what I'll dream tonight. Context has duration, as in the continuous present of political protest, whose outcome is never assured and whose cause, affixed to ambient conditions, contains simultaneously both its past and its future. I dream that I'm a resident of a hotel in Bombay, a hotel run by a family whose previous hotel was in Africa. I lived in that one for a time, too. The beautiful and enchanting little daughter is crying; she thinks I don't like her. But I love her, I say to her father. Yes, he says, it would be impossible not to. It's easier to draw an admonition than a moral from a dream when it's one's own. How does one care about the things one knows? Why does one come to care, and how does one carry out the caring? Maxims: Leave the sparrows singing in the bush and let your tears of laughter add salt to the sea. The man who runs uphill will eventually run down. Money may make a man but what it makes him may not be worth much. It's not shame that binds us to duty but beauty. A chant goes up: Indict the kleptocrats! Every political action carries out an interpretation of what has preceded it. Let's rename the great public university on whose campus the students are chanting, and let's relocate it. There; we've done it. History has to have something to start with. Martin Jay, borrowing terminology from Claude Romano's Event and World, refers to events that re-open history as "advents." They are "like what Nietzsche called 'lightning flashes,' which are radical breaks in the status quo...inaugurating their own future, as advents that open up possible adventures in a future not yet determined." The university might now occupy a hillside on the habitable planet that Earthling astronomers refer to as P72e3 and its American administrators call Consolation (or Conso®). What the native inhabitants of P72e3 call the site remains a mystery; P72e3ese is impossible to translate into English, as it's a language of "radical non-indexicality." The grammar is stable (as far as we can tell), but the word-units that fill out the grammar seem to change meaning from one moment to the next and arbitrarily. Any word might mean anything at any given instant. No dictionary of the language is possible; evaluations are possible but never stick. What's hip one minute might be foot another, what's chill might turn pocket, uniform, speck, stick, changeling, dope. Indeed, on P72e3 it is impossible to know what it might mean to turn. The P72e3lings appear simultaneously aggressive and agreeable. Do they or don't they want to adapt to the new social conditions? We need glossy advertisements for life. As the cricket says, Live it, live it, live it. Moral: Life is to be lived. Rating of moral: Widely applicable but with local restrictions. Unrestricted application of moral: Insane vivacity, exhaustion, possible dismay. Reality is full of problems. They exist objectively, independent of our being troubled by, or fascinated by, or drawn into them. And they aren't all sites of divisiveness; problem-solving isn't necessarily accomplished by identifying a problem and its elements and then separating ourselves from them or them from each other. Problems can exist as compilations, their elements drawn together by a compelling (and neither unifying nor homogenizing) force that overrides, or perhaps creates, the problem as such. Most social relations are problems. "I've used half a tube of titanium white on this," says Lily Ball. "The value of a painting is determined by how much one can get someone to pay for it," says Tamarind Magee. "Nothin' 'bout time and materials," says Commando. "Nothin' 'bout cuttin', erasin', drawin', and tellin' it like it is." "No one gets paid just for living," says Tamarind. "How do you think I should sign my name?" asks Rosario Basho Clark, gesturing with a paintbrush toward the canvas board the others can see only the back of. No one answers. Not every work of art has a future. More to the point, not every work of art can produce a future. As Melville's Ishmael notes in an early chapter of Moby-Dick, "We are too much like oysters observing the sun through water." "I'll try Rio," says Rosario. Rosario Basho Clark, Lily Ball, Commando, and Tamarind Magee occupy one of many possible presents. It is there ——— which is to say, then ——— that I picture them in the scuffed but not tawdry milieu of a class-room. Several large tables sit in the middle of the room, there are shelves along one wall, large-paned dirty wood frame win-dows along another, drawings and paintings hang in view, several vividly painted papier-mâché sculptures are arrayed on a shelf ——— it is the "art room" of the converted warehouse in which the Oakland MAP is located (not far from Frank Ogawa/ Oscar Grant Plaza, the site of ongoing political protests). "In this day and age, everyday life is lit by false suns: morality, the state, ideology. They bathe it in a phoney light, and even worse, they lower it to the depths where possibilities cannot be per-ceived, and keep it there. Sadly, the stars of what is possible shine only at night." Rosario has been working at an upright easel. He turns the easel so the others can see the painting's phenomenological face, a surface on which expectation has passed through experience and produced memories. An alle-gorical situation arises, in what Rosalind Krauss has called "the space of confrontation between the sign or emblem and the one who views it." Such a space, she says, is created by "a directive addressed to someone, who is asked to make sense of it." Its propositional open-endedness is of crucial importance. As Barbara Maria Stafford, in her book Visual Analogy, puts it, "a proposition [...] is an offer extended by one body or thing to another inviting it to relate in a new manner." But who are these characters for whom I've invented names? Or perhaps that's the wrong question. Rather: what are these names for which I might invent characters: Gloria Steven Nakamura, Vivienne Forty Shushanian, Blister O'Leary March, Kasper Anselm Vanderenden, Xialu Janet Wang, Legs Nadler Lexington? These are possible names for credible configurations that, emerging from a collision of contexts, might show up in a work of documentary prose. They are, I assure you, based on actual people; they transfer one reality to another. Events need to be connected, and we prefer them to be connected to humans (though connections to other creatures can often be delightful and pertinent, as in La Fontaine's Fables, for example). Connections to inanimate existence are harder to care about. Minerals are connected to geologists. But perhaps I'm wrong about that ———— maybe geologists are connected to minerals. We like to give characters a landscape to inhabit. Clark Kent, Peter Parker ———— they leapt out of a landscape to undertake acts of heroism. Marcel Proust, James Joyce, Herman Melville, Marianne Moore, Willa Cather ———— they burrowed into one. Sunlight is sliding over the street and bouncing on the whitecaps the wind is pushing across the bay; it spreads along the piers and strikes the façades of buildings in the financial district it cannot enter. "Who comes is occupied" ———— thus begins the tenth poem of George Oppen's Discrete Series. The poet is watching a steam shovel operator engrossed in his task; he is stripping away a stretch of pavement or road, leaving "The asphalt edge / loose on the plateau," and exposing what seems to be a rapid sequence of earlier moments there ———— an unfettered horse, sparks from an electric streetcar, the images themselves lasting no longer than one of the sparks. Under the pavement and asphalt surfaces of Education Alley, College Avenue, Enlightenment Street, Mobility Boulevard, Anxiety Lane lies gray or dun-colored dirt, hard-packed and inert, reeking of dead bacteria, deprived of sunlight and rain, oppressed by the weight of the city. The sun moves relentlessly, slowly but without caution; with each change of position, it withdraws its light from one thing and casts it onto the next, allegorizing and then de-allegorizing and then re-allegorizing again. Continuity is made, not found. But is it really, as Kierkegaard suggests, only human beings that can consciously enter into continuities, only they who, by hoping for a future, can "gain a history"? Images of clocks and watches ——— in advertisements, films, photo-graphs, paintings, literature ("The clock was striking. The leaden circles dissolved in the air") ——— create anxiety rather than continuity, a sense of time's reluctance to approach or its inabil-ity to withdraw. Whatever the time that the face of the clock or watch registers, even if it happens to be the same time it is now, it is nonetheless that time at some other time than this one. The present is a tense of multiple, alternative hours. They don't accumulate and can't be gathered together, but they aren't inconsequential. Though they are so closely intercon-nected in the popular imagination, heroism and history offer us materials from which we can extrapolate very different mean-ings. True, history produces heroes, and heroes produce history; or, perhaps, history just happens and heroics are opportunistic, or accidental. The heroes of this text (only glimpsed, but palpa-ble in their effect) are perhaps like Dr. Rieux in Camus's novel The Plague; they take the requisite actions because there's no good reason not to. These are the grounds on which they dis-cover their ethical and practical imperatives. Heroism is in a praxis, just as victory is in a struggle. What heroes do is per-fectly ordinary. Heroism, like history, can never deem anything insignificant. But what of Nikolai Rostov, the eager young brother of the heroine of War and Peace, whose first encounter with battle is overridden by the accidental. His account of it, accurately told, would be of nothing but trivia. Everything hap-pened not as he willed it, but as if directed by accident. And so, likewise, is his account. "He could not simply tell them that they all set out at a trot, he fell off his horse, dislocated his arm, and ran to the woods as fast as he could to escape a Frenchman." Perhaps we are as little in control of our interpretations of his-tory as we are of history itself. Tolstoy tells us that young Nikolai "began telling the story with the intention of telling it exactly as it had been, but imperceptibly, involuntarily, and inevitably for himself, he went over into untruth." And with that untruth Nikolai creates an image appropriate to the silent caption he imagines underwriting the battle experience he wishes he had had: "A Young Hero at Dawn," "On the Road to Victory," or, simply, "Courage."

Armbands, tie on the red
Behind, half the citizenry left
Black, wearing
Cap, military cunt
Day, livelong
Direction, the right
Doors into another world, let's open
Exits, entrances should reverse
Happiness, quotidian
Implacable, remain
In arms, comrades
Pathos, historical
Silence, in a confounding
Silence, keep
Tension, unbreakable
Us, they are threatening
Victorious, patience will make us
You, thank
Yourself, do it
Wound, head

If you want to point something out, you should be neither too close to it nor too far away. If, however, you find yourself in the latter situation, please note that things that are far away are easier to point out if they are moving.

11

People speak of false starts. Jumping the gun, coming to a conceptual dead end, getting nowhere. In the wake of the false start, it's assumed that a better start will take place, a true beginning, whose success lies in its continuing on until it comes to its proper conclusion and brings something about. Stray ideas, then settlement, gymnastics, topographical maps, similes, a hardboiled egg ——— a real egg, still warm, chopped, and spread on a slice of buttered sourdough toast ——— all unabstracted from their common material context: a summer morning, a specific one, which, like a dream, holds out incidents under tension. Water is spilling onto the floor. A hole breaks open in the ceiling, and gooey, acrid, wet plaster falls on my face. I open my mouth to say something ——— what would I have said? ——— globs of the goo fall into my mouth. I bend forward and vomit into my hands. This season, which is fast disappearing, will not turn out to have been a tell-all time. But for awhile during it everything was permissible ——— lies, fake IDs, polylingual melodramas, an invasion of pantry moths. Much of everyday life (murmuring repetition) goes on invisibly, including the tendency to fantasize, to plan or perseverate, to feel oneself to be in the right or in the wrong, to imagine changes (or changing). Even to dream of insurrection, or to live contradictorily, against one's class background, say, and against one's education, and pretending to be, like many tellers of tales, born from the dark and the daughter of a goose. Detlev Claussen, writing about Adorno, says, "The idea of happiness continues to live off the ahistorical moment of the absence of contradiction." Such an idea (or experience) of happiness emerges from one's being in accord with whatever happens ——— from one's amor fati. It is a form, albeit an active one, of fatalism. There's no reason to take fatalism here in a solely derogatory sense. But "all's for the best" is not synonymous with "all's for happiness" or "all provides happiness." Everyday life (shafts of repetition) is a matter of brute force and great delicacy.

Invalid invalid, whose content now
Contends with will and will not lamely bow
To anyone, not even banker thiefs
Whose weight in gold has crushed the coral reefs.

What of the false halt? It would be a halt that's incompatible with what began, though what began is now the site of the halt. It's an unwarranted halt, extraneous and imposed on something that was underway. What has been begun encounters something off-putting, collides with some consequential stupidity, experiences (whether directly or indirectly) some trauma, arrives at an impasse or impediment, and is beset with apathy, exhaustion, and ———— and this is my point ———— fear. The mind closes, thought leaps backward and plunges into itself, withdrawing from the world in whose realities it has been accustomed to ponder, calculate, remember, combine, scan and map, dream. A false halt occurs at a moment of decontextualization, when history is stripped away by fear. That said, it should not be assumed that historians are fearless, nor that the present tense is timid. What clings to the present tense is a certain aura of exemplarity, not of personage but of situation, so that it isn't, for example, Leo X. Lee's and Russell Wright's constantly interrupted progress through the day but the interruptedness itself that can be read as an epitome of (since they are musicians) musicianship, or of aesthetic progress (as if there were such a thing), or of my efforts to write this book. Along comes sudden sunlight, intruding on my attention: sudden sunlit intrusion. Sun on inanimate objects that determine my experience of the day: sun on a striped glass of orange juice, on a pair of scuffed flat misshapen (or reshaped to my needs) black shoes, sun on my veined and mottled right hand, sun on the newspaper.

BAY EXPERTS SAY BRIDGE BOLTS SAFE
WHISTLE BLOWER'S ANONYMITY BLOWN
REBELS STARVED FOR ARMS
IS POTATO GROUP PUMPING SPUD PRICES UP?
FORECLOSURE EVERYTHING CONFUSING CAN MAKE

Ellie North Roth, enjoying the liberating prospects of her increasing old age, suddenly says to Albert Sing Roth, "I'm never going to wear high-heeled shoes again. Or ——— actually ——— what I mean is that I don't care." Albert Sing Roth can't so easily cast aside the future possibilities that Ellie regards as past restrictions. He rises heavily ——— though until that very moment he was feeling light, buoyant, cheerful ——— and stumbles very slightly, as an old man might, or as an old man just did, he says to himself. Behind the house is a little fenced-in yard, home to a scrappy, shadowy garden of shaggy ferns, tattered foxglove, and cineraria stalks whose flower heads have gone to seed. A more courageous writer might sow her texts more densely with commas. If a chain of associations starts here, why not follow it as it clanks and clatters through dismal banalities, indignities, and self-betrayals? It is only through the presence of others, all in their own constellations of facts, that possessiveness can yield to combination. Can late style ——— the artistic style of the artist in old age ——— cut the materials of experience free from the possessively inventive imagination? Writing to Walter Benjamin in 1940, Adorno said, "For all reification is forgetting: objects become purely thing-like the moment they are retained for us without the continued presence of their other aspects: when something of them has been forgotten." Memories thrust experiences back into time, but not back into reality. Memory and history expose us to contradictory pasts. One is a not-past past, a past that hasn't gone past, hasn't passed, the so-called living past. This should be distinguished from another, a past that wasn't passed ——— the past that wasn't experienced. And that past is different from the past that hasn't been passed at all, a past that hasn't yet been lived through, the unperceived past in which one is trapped. Time includes the past, but human memory and human history has only an unpast. Perhaps the clearest manifestation of a leap out of a leap out of time is the nightmare. Or perhaps not. Ambiguities everywhere should be collected as evidence of ambivalence. But I've been arrested for falling asleep; I'm guilty of being tired. It's late and there's only one small room left in the hotel. I check in and follow the bellhop ——— he's wearing chains on his legs ——— to my cell. I tip him ——— I have hidden a dollar bill tucked into my sleeve. "Be

my guest," he says. He hands me a glutinous, cold dead baby
——— the future ——— and screams. In Paco David Fantine's
seminar paper "On the Poetics of Witness," he writes, "Last
year riot police beat friends and mentors in a university demon-
stration I was too afraid to stand in." He goes on to elaborate
on what he calls the phenomenology of his fear, and of not wit-
nessing the beatings, but of witnessing his not witnessing the
beatings as the event of his fear ——— the witnessing of his
abjection. Fear is a condition of sheer, unmitigated interiority.
To be afraid is to sink into abyssal subjectivity. The best rem-
edy for it is, in my experience, o comrades, camaraderie. So
says an orator, too stubborn to admit defeat, through a bullhorn.
The crowd at the noon hour rally is small. Standing near the
platform, Jillie Jane Rogers feels incongruous, alienated, then
decisively foolhardy. At the playground, Antonia Alice Martin
won't try the rings because she's afraid of blisters. Waving both
hands through the air, she says she's <u>not</u> afraid of <u>things</u>. The
distinction is a strange one, the product of fantastical objectifi-
cation, producing a sense of vivid vulnerability. At the rally, Jillie
Jane Rogers's spirits have retreated, and then come out again.
The students are weary, but not world-weary; they are not the
romantics of their time. Jillie Jane Rogers considers the lines of
logic on her clipboard. "Verses tremble, shaken / like sycamores
by alliteration." There are sycamore trees at the edge of the
plaza, their shadows nervous. Love, hate, excitement, curiosity
can be performed (and also, therefore, simulated), commercial-
ized, commodified. And war ——— has it been commodified?
It is merchandized, but in ways that are peculiar to contempo-
rary modes of commercialization: the bourgeois citizenry has to
be sold on it, and then they can be sold news of it. Exchanges
happen in a war, but, except insofar as "cannon fodder" is cash
of a certain kind and populations are capital, they are only con-
tingently related to exchange-value in the Marxist sense. But
wars have enormous, though never unlimited, news-value. Leo
X. Lee fakes prowess, Tamarind Magee fakes power, Flip fakes
attitude. Everyone's a hero, says Samantha Bell Chow. Then
no one is, says Nicholas Declan Callahan, no one. No predica-
tion stands alone: she stands, he drinks, they travel, it spreads
its leaves, it stalks a mouse, she stands again. Actions point to

agents, agents point to actions. The haphazards of adventure are never over. "Flies seem to experience the motion of my hand, fast as it is, as a slow arrival that allows them plenty of time to fly away."

12

Just to set out to write impressions arbitrarily derived from details of a day should keep one alert to sensations and perceptions. We are not the only gatherers. A flock of blackbirds swirls over the supermarket parking lot, then settles along the long front edge of the building's roof, peeping and buzzing, endlessly shifting position. With each sensation we detect a detail on the basis of which we interpret and become better informed. But that's not enough. Attention is no longer a sufficient or meaningful aesthetic principle, though it was one once. To the extent that an avant-garde nowadays might produce an aesthetic, it would have to do so in response to its assessment of society and, concomitantly, to its evaluation of itself as a social phenomenon. An individual may love privacy or fear publicity, but at the moment in which she or he makes art in the context of an avant-garde, he or she does so as a social being. The term "avant-garde" can never properly be applied to a solitary artist, working individually. It is never legitimately an identity, a mode of personhood. And it can't become an instrument for enhancing self-consciousness, since self-consciousness is always stagnant ———— or, perhaps it's more accurate to say that self-consciousness is a condition of stagnation. One six pack of Thomas' Sourdough English Muffins, value $4.29, 130 calories per muffin. .71 lb of Niman Ranch ground beef, value $6.38. One 12-ounce jar of Stonewall Kitchen blood orange marmalade, value $6.99. ½ pound Challenge sweet butter, value $4.47, 100 calories per tablespoon. 1 lb Barilla spaghetti, $2.17, 1600 calories per box. One package (12 count) La Tortilla Factory king size corn tortillas, $2.99, 65 calories each. One head red leaf lettuce, $1.99. One cucumber, 69 cents. Two zucchini (.56 lb), $1.11. One yellow onion (.57 lb), 39 cents. One enumerates for lack of anything else to do, or one enumerates to locate, as a surveyor might. A young woman is sitting on the ground in the cold June sunlight just outside the entrance to the market. Her back is against the wall, her legs stretched out in front of her, her lunch on her lap. As I approach her, I venture a tentative smile; she glares, she takes an aggressive bite of her sandwich, and with lips slightly parted, she chews. "The earth moves on from day to night; the individual dies, but the sun itself burns without intermission, an eternal noon," as the pessimistic Schopenhauer says. I don't deny I had a childhood, a period of powerlessness I didn't recognize as powerless. I know I screamed and went rigid in the event, that was a trick I learned through imitation of figures that no simile could match, consternations fizzling and tumbling in the skull, foreshadows of insistence that I would try later to enunciate but which remained ineffectual, forming the inscrutable background to misrepresentation, misunderstanding. History can make even the happiest person miserable. A heroine tests her freedom by strolling from stem to stern and back to stem again, through the weeds and over the sea at the end of an old fantasy, the start of a new. Or so it goes in the familiar tale called <u>An Argument or Argonautessa</u>, and the moment just ahead is now anxiously awaiting its turn. The Greek gods didn't age, but they did experience loss. Fear of loss (sparking jealousy) and experience of loss (causing rage) informed many of their mythic interventions into the historical (time-bound) world. The pendulum swings, the hands are motionless. A bit of ceased existence has arrived. And meanwhile one moment becomes the next without any apparent break. "Don't noodle with your peas," Askari Nate Martin says to Antonia. "Dad, that's awesome," says Jonah, reaching for his water glass, "Get it? Noodling with peas and then peeing on...?" "That's not awesome, it's awful," says Malaya, gathering her thick hair at the back of her neck and pulling it out of her way. "In case you're interested," she adds, "the volleyball assistant told us today that Charles Fourier called family meals lugubrious." Malaya Martin is no longer entirely oblivious of the shape of the puzzle piece that she occupies and wants to occupy it fully. Askari Nate Martin knows that the puzzle extends in every direction infinitely and remains silent. But of course: the Askari Nate Martin of this tale is subject to desires so intimate that he is scarcely aware of them. On the kitchen counter behind him sits a red bowl, a band of late sunlight slips over its glazed round lip and suddenly illuminates the three lemons, perfect grapefruit, five tangerines with short dark stems and small brittle leaves, and a single lime. Are Bonnard's paintings about form and rhyme? They aren't about surface. You could say that everything in them —— especially in the late interiors —— has fleeting existence, but the paintings are not about time. And they aren't about space; their stunning effects depend not on perspective but on juxtapositions, most of them so soft they overcome boundaries, dis-edge entities, disclosing the incremental and contingent qualities of their existence. The worlds of transition are ones of microcosmic shifts, quivers, responses to minute pressures. A close observer of a Bonnard painting, like a vigilant astronomer, will participate in the transitions that perception makes rather than the stabilities that comprise the things they perceive. He paints depth liberated from perspective —— the abyss of violet strokes hovering among yellows. Allen Grossman has argued that perspective in the visual arts was originally a class-based device, reflecting an upper class world view. The upper classes could see into the distance; they had prospects. The working classes, meanwhile, lived and worked in tiny, confined spaces, in spaces without prospects. They didn't possess distance. The lecture in which Grossman was developing this argument was on William Blake; being of the working class, as Grossman pointed out, William Blake refused to utilize perspective. But there are other reasons to show flatness in the world, to show distance without temporality. Bonnard was solidly middle-class, and it isn't class consciousness but awareness of death that drew him first to the non-perspectival intensity of color. It's a question —— political these day, but aesthetic too (as it was in Bonnard's day) —— of endings; we want to know what's relevant, ultimately, when it comes to endings, not least because we ourselves have brought about too many of them. We need proprioceptive skills to assess our approach to ends and to endings, our own included. They bring us to thresholds, on which we teeter, not sure of the degree of our tilt or the speed at which we are falling or causing other things to do so. The intermediate irritations, anxieties, frustrations, regrets are all at odds with serenity and evidence of failure. And then accusation —— and especially self-accusation —— resounds as a form of judgment. It's exhausting. And yet attentiveness is an obligation. The thing to avoid here is surveillance, putting one-self at a spy's distance from others. History can make even the happiest person terrible. Nothing can counter this. Everything has to be seen a thousand times and once, perhaps against an ochre background, or a field of modulating blue, from the seat of a yellow Mercury convertible, top down, sweeping under dangling pungent eucalyptus leaves so as to feel the breeze. This was my father's idea, a message I'm sure we understood, coded as it was in the Cold War vernacular, clearly defiant, an open message but to interpretation. Interpretation is yet to get it. If there's no chronicle except the record of one's thoughts, memories, ideas, then there's no reality but in the practice of it, with sensations, awareness of right foot, tone in ears, pleas-ant sunny hue to the paint on the walls, messages taken <u>cum grano salis</u>.

13

The danger is that we don't think the obvious. The result is ide-
ology. Helplessly, hope prevails. We live on a curve. Or we live
within circumscribed limits, assailed by curves. Everyday life
(loosened repetition) is immersed in ideology, suffused with
fantasy, but in itself everyday life (stuttering repetition) can't
be fantasized. People have experiences collectively but also,
and simultaneously, separately. As I lie awake, I can hear the
hum of electricity, which is the hum of accelerating wakeful-
ness, or perhaps it's a layer of dreaming. Aficionados of the in-
ternet, meanwhile, entertain the fantasy that it is or will be the
site of universal knowledge, global social relations, and mental
freedom. Skeptics see it as a site of pseudo-connectivity ———
bondage ——— and social engineering. Skeptics regard it as
capitalism's most powerful instrument to date; this too may be
a fantasy. Fantasies are an expression of the desire for order,
which they yearn to impose on what otherwise exists only in po-
tentia. It is through our fantasies that we allow ourselves to in-
dulge in our most grandiose scenarios of control. There is no
plan that's not a social fantasy. Every plan, in other words, en-
tails a plot. The figure of a man, Samuel Wang Xie, appears out
of nowhere, standing in a city park in which every blade of grass,
every bush, all the other men and women and children, the
parked cars, the yarrow, every pebble on the path, an abandoned
jacket, a blue jay in a pine tree, and every leaf are all equally in
the foreground. Our attention is magnetized. Nothing recedes.
No vanishing point offers itself, nothing can move out of focus.
"Without my swearing to it, you can believe that I would like this
book, the child of my understanding, to be the most beautiful,
the most brilliant, and the most discreet that anyone could
imagine." Such is the first sentence (in Edith Grossman's trans-
lation) of Don Quixote. Events slip between other events; we live
as insertions, twitch, laugh, yield slightly, shove ahead. Both the
raising and the razing of cities with their playgrounds and store-
fronts and housing projects coexist; children at play remain in

the city plaza or park, as does the hour elsewhere of their wanton slaughter. There isn't much time for reflection. I sit over in a corner of the room on the second floor watching and listening to the window, amazed at the gusts of vernal wind and the shaking of the glass. "Steel-blue and light, ruffled by a soft, scarcely perceptible cross-wind, the waves of the Adriatic streamed against the imperial squadron as it steered toward the harbor of Brundisium, the flat hills of the Calabrian coast coming gradually nearer on the left." This, in Jean Starr Untermeyer's translation, is the first sentence of Hermann Broch's The Death of Virgil, written in a German concentration camp in 1938. Virgil's last attempt at conversation breaks off: "To the child..." ——— his speech ends without a period. Perhaps societies die similarly. If we want to imagine a university as something akin to an ant colony, we have to concede that there's no egg-producing queen at its center. The queens ——— and they are multiple ——— are off-site, producing future students, future faculty, future staff. A university is a colony without a queen, then, but with multiple workers (of different castes but not predestined to their roles by gender) and some drones. None of the workers attend to a queen, but all are expected to attend to the progeny of queens. To escape boredom, May-Marie Channing looks for something to do. Does she want a distraction, something to preoccupy her so that she can let time go by without feeling distress? Or does she want to find something that she can contribute to time, something that will establish the period as hers, transforming it into memorable time, time added to her life? She can't know in advance what the effect will be of whatever it is she finds to do. The forecast in yesterday's newspaper predicting that today would be clear, sunny, and warm was wrong, the product of an erroneous view of the (near) future. The misbegotten prediction, however, doesn't generate an aporia around predictions of a ceasefire, of waterfront turmoil, of a hockey victory, of economic trends. There are citizens in some parts of the world who read the news as I read cartoon strips. And every evening the people in the city of Z grieve for one to two hours over all the crimes committed that day everywhere on earth. Moving at night through the alleyways between buildings, a group of deserters makes its way out of the city and then disbands. When will I again find myself thinking of C? In winter? Tomorrow? When I'm folding laundry? When I am next in Edinburgh? It is in the salutary failure of timelessness in art that art and the everyday recover their reciprocal uncertainty, with art reinvigorated by relevance even at a material level and the everyday reinvigorated by the presence throughout it of singularities. What's at stake for experience and hence for art, to the degree that art is affixed, conceptually and practically, to experience, is a long struggle with time. What do we do with the time we have? As Viktor Shklovsky says, "Art itself is constructed on the notion that history isn't predictable, it's unexpected because it's not a myth." In a forest in France, an American woman is out for a walk with a French friend. Birds are singing, and suddenly both women understand what the birds are saying. To the American woman they seem to be speaking in English, while they seem to the French woman to speak in French. But natural knowledge is not universal, and the two women are told very different things. To the degree that the everyday is resistant to any universal narrative (and to find evidence that it is so, one has only to consider, for example, how fundamentally unquotidian Wagner's mythic universalism is), the everyday —— if and when it is consciously taken up as a practice —— might be deemed counter-historical. What it counters with is everything that's happening in the context of all that has happened —— history in particulate form. Its methods are tactical, furtive, just as allegories are furtive. All-that-is-happening can only be thought as the substrate of a poetics of history, just as poetics is the constructive fantasy of poetry. Its products —— strange kinds of knowledge —— are not <u>mere</u> fantasy. The word "mere" is a semantic intensifier, and despite the fact that what we think it intensifies is triviality, what it intensifies, properly speaking, is the suchness of that which it qualifies, as the qualified per se —— its being nothing more or other than what it is. The word comes from the Latin <u>merus</u>, meaning "unmixed," "pure"; its Indo-European root is <u>*mer-</u>, to sparkle. It is not, however, because the elements in a fantasy retain an eye-catching quality that we so frequently term them "mere." Though we cannot know whether to believe the report, an astronautical robot ——the Mars Phoenix Lander —— is said to have found "water ice" in "the low-lying Northern plains" of Mars. With such phrases, Mars is being made familiar to us. The way is being prepared for us to consider it as a possible home. Now as in the past, to look for a lost civilization is to look for that civilization's dim future in the present. Perhaps our own civilization is merely an image of a civilization, flat as a projection on a screen. We don't live it, but we can observe it, and we probably ought to do so. I am watching myself closely. "That's been the old philosophical injunction since Plato," says Derrida: "to philosophize is to learn to die." If so, the poetic injunction wants to redirect that of philosophy, prompting us to learn to live. And Montaigne would argue that a proper philosophy allows us to live without fear of dying. There was a time when the certainty that I would see my perpetual beloved on the following Saturday afternoon made me impatient for the intervening days to cascade immediately, in a single swift unit, into the past, but worry that that certainty wasn't certain at all made the hours crawl over the intervening surface of time as slowly as glass sagging downward in a window pane. I pondered the possibility —— merely hypothetical, an impossibility in fact —— that time might finally congeal and petrify, that a moment would come that wouldn't go by. This wouldn't be a Nietzschean eternal return of the same but simply an eternal same. We'd freeze, as in a game of "statue." Would we ache to move, I wondered, or would our thoughts be frozen too. I could have asked myself what it would be like to feel as I'm feeling just now forever, but I didn't know what I was feeling. I remember throwing an orange plastic toy across the meadow for the dog; the toy sailed in a long, high arc and the dog dashed after it, leaping over the grass, tail flying behind her —— she was utterly beautiful. There are no social relations that aren't also fantastic. "Having before him a four-month wait for a position he had been promised, he looked around for some means of occupying his time and hit upon the idea of searching for a way to make all men happy." A pleasant father chuckles amorously, like one bird responding to another, as his little daughter at his side chatters about this and that. Because I love you, you are honest, wise, intelligent, and beautiful. Let's indulge in what Susan Buck-Morss terms "capriciousness of meaning," while bearing in mind, as she says, that its exercise needs "to be critically understood, not blindly affirmed." It is with notable capriciousness that death provides the context in which a final judgment as to the happiness or goodness of a life is to be judged. Montaigne quotes Ovid as the authority for the idea that death evaluates life. "In everything else there may be sham: the fine reasonings of philosophy may be a mere pose in us [...]. But in the last scene, between death and ourselves, there is no more pretending." In the final disenchanting of the world, attention turns entirely to the present. Interpretation falls away. But it hasn't yet. She is one, he is one, you is one, I is one, fetched and crossing a dull moment with tremulous pleasure. Day: experiential; noon: narcotic; midnight: inextricable; late June: inevitable. They say that poetry will sabotage an anonymous tyranny, but which, among so many, they don't say. The aphoristic game is like musical chairs. In the end, only one aphorism is left, not the best or truest but the luckiest, the one closest to the last chair when the music stops. Social changes move more slowly than words. But they do so more broadly. Language narrows a change, focuses it ——— but it is in the nature of change that it not be narrow or focused. Is it with Socrates or with Romanticism that Western humans first began to ask themselves how they are feeling? Certainly the Greeks were well-acquainted with the concept (and presumably the experience) of well-being. It nestles in a web of needs. Along the principal commercial block in the neighborhood there are thirty-eight shops, twenty on the east side of the street and eighteen on the west. The shops on the east side are flanked by a bank at one end and a candy shop at the other. The needs these two establishments fulfill are not incommensurate. Across the street from a wine shop, on the west side of the street, is a luxury ice cream shop, which, if one counts it as an eating establishment, is one of six on the block, which harbors three restaurants, a coffee shop, and a delicatessen with a few tables. Apart from the bank, the only establishments supplying what might be called practical necessities are a dry cleaner, a stationery shop, two shoe shops, the (very expensive) delicatessen, and four clothing shops. There's a book shop; presumably it caters to intellectual or entertainment needs. The rest of the small businesses (three jewelry shops, several gift shops, a pet shop specializing in birds, etc.) cater to aesthetic and/or frivolous needs ——— or, as is the case with the several gift shops, the cafes, the wine shop, to social needs. Susan Buck-Morss, writing on Walter Benjamin's Arcades Project, comments, "The vibrancy of collective fantasy is a crucial indicator of the healthy development of these needs." This neighborhood shopping district for the most part attracts a casual or sociable clientele, as well as residents who use the bank and cleaner and the post office in the next block. The development of people's needs is determined only in part by the level of difficulty they encounter when trying to satisfy them, while the health of that development, as of the needs themselves and the neighborhood, is determined by the degree to which they can be satisfied in a non-predatory way. The general claim these days is that everyday life (passing repetition) is being withdrawn from reality and reconstituted virtually; it's being relocated to a screen. There one plays it, as if it were a game. Or one responds to it, as if it were a stream of messages bearing ideas and demands and invitations and requests that together constitute a sea of obligations bound together by desires and duties that bind us to them, in turn. Every plot, including a plot of land, is a narrative zone; topology is the study of plots. Clint Eastwood in "Blood Work" (and certain other of his later films) has invented a new romantic role, into which he casts himself. It is the figure of the all-but-decrepit old man. His health is precarious, his abilities diminished; he is physically and psychologically vulnerable. And yet he proves to be invincible: an invincible (i.e. essentially immortal) hero marred (romanticized) by the signs of mortality. In "Blood Work," we expect him to lose heart (to lose his heart) at any moment, but, since courage and good-heartedness are synonymous for this hero, he keeps it. By the end of the movie, he has, however, detached himself from the male-bound world. His former buddy, aptly named Buddy, is cast aside, since, in an unexpected turn of the plot, Buddy turns out to have been the killer our knocked-about codger has been pursuing, and Eastwood becomes the lover, but also the sister, of the woman who initially hired him, and mother to the murder victim's child. A life has multiple "conceptual centers" (to use another of Susan Buck-Morss's terms). They aren't mutually exclusive.

14

Children love color, but even more they love sculpting ———— whether they do it by pushing and patting sand, or plucking handfuls of grass, or by squeezing soft food, or collecting pebbles or buttons or Legos or pyracanthus berries in a bucket, or by carving patterns into pudding. This must be primordial behavior. Each continent sits in its own separate sea, one of wine, one of cream, one of melted butter, one of lime juice, one of vinegar, one of tea, and one of ever-falling rain water. Those who are native to the continent surrounded by cream traditionally worship cumulous clouds, which they regard as divinities, continuously changing form. I know this is sad, but sadness is a pervasive, though perhaps strange, form of continuity. A divinity may be briefly an exhausted soldier, or a rumpled gray calf at the udder of a diminishing cow. And now for a few days the current batch of political candidates have disappeared from the front page of the daily newspaper, replaced by coverage of spreading drought and mandatory water rationing (we are required to reduce our water consumption by 19%), a devastating earthquake in China, the deteriorating post-cyclone situation in Burma/Myanmar. Mikhail Epstein has coined the word chronophilia; it refers to compulsive attention to the continuous flow of broadcast news, producing in the chronophile the sense, if not the reality, that he or she is a witness to time itself, forming into events. Of these events, however, the chronophile, within a day or two, can remember nothing. They pass through chronophiliac temporality without adhering to anything. The chronophile's time gets filled up and remains empty. The sun is a locked door. The weather is warm, a pigeon flying from one roof to another utters a peep with each beat of its wings, someone in the neighborhood is deftly wielding a hammer, striking with regular blows. The nail goes neatly into the wood and the board is bound to the stud. Here's a typical bit of fiction: Jane walked down her front stairs onto Russell Street, worrying that the phone message from Timmy's school was summoning her to be informed of yet another "problematic concern." Across the street, James, thinking about the beginning of his shift, noticed her coming out of the house and waved. He was surprised when she didn't acknowledge his greeting. Who could possibly know all this? The "omniscient voice" of narrative fiction is the most bizarre invention still at play in the arts, and, despite its frequent deployment in so called "realist" fiction, it unfolds at an unfathomable distance from actual, consciously-lived reality. It's fantastic! But what if an author doesn't want to reach the audience in the expected way? The major north-south streets running through the center of the city might be an Earlier Street, an Improbable Avenue, a Later Avenue, and a Remarkable Boulevard. Crossing these might run various smaller streets, given over to residential buildings and small shops: an Erstwhile Lane, a Systematizing Street, an Uncompromising Street, a Possible Alley. Coming from work, I find that my usual route home along Closest Road is cut off by police activity ——— black and white patrol cars block access. I don't know what has happened and want to. In Bernadette Mayer's Memory, there is always a hint, a suggestion, a possibility (none of which are proper to memory as we conventionally think of it but all of which nonetheless haunt it) that she is preparing to rob a bank or stick up a convenience store. But to a large degree, the world of everyday life (resident repetition) is independent of invention; it's given. Christa Wolf (in One Day a Year) speaks of "the growing uneventfulness of modernity" and "modern man's neediness, which is often hidden, even from himself." Everyday life is lived at a mesocosmic level ——— it's almost never viewed close-up (in detail) nor from a distance (as a set of changing patterns). It is said that hummingbirds migrate by riding geese. This isn't true. For a writer of bourgeois inwardness, the highest achievements are dreams. Reading through the first issue of a xeroxed literary journal published in Ciudad Juarez, I find half the pages covered with a language I don't understand, but I imagine I can. My demons tell me that the heart stands guard in fish over those who breathe. Nothing is incidental. If everyday life (thudding repetition) can't be invented, perhaps it can be inventoried. Here is an alphabetical index to some local billboards:

Authenticity, choose
Billboard, this isn't a
Car, America's most fuel-efficient
Chuck, talk to
Fees, death by a thousand
Happiness, don't keep bottled up
Hippies, Yuppies and Yippies, full coverage for
Motherland, fresh from the
Outlet, everybody needs an
Plant, it's not a power
Results, call us for great
Savings, big
Twist, give your summer a
World, oceans are part of your

I pass some doors that open onto other hallways; the names of the rooms available via each door are etched on them, but I can't find the access to Room K. I go back outside and walk down the street toward a large department store, Kissiwick. Room K. And my bag is empty —— completely empty; I've been pickpocketed. My black leather backpack has nothing in it. There is a degree of happiness, very close to unhappiness but not quite it yet, that comes to the dutiful, the obedient. The soil holds the roots of the plants, the plants hold up the sky, and we walk through it —— this is how it is described. The world of fish is an imperfect analogy to it. Viktor Shklovsky says, "It seems that in order to have a new society there has to be a shipwreck." Is this what George Oppen was thinking when, in his poem "Of Being Numerous," he speaks of "the shipwreck of the singular"? A jay squawks, birds twitter. One can't look at the sun unaided, one has to use something intermediary whose function is precisely to partially obscure the sun. The next morning's predawn pink tint is not a source of light but its seeming destination, and as the tint receives the rising sun it fades —— or retreats —— or doesn't fade but is obliterated. Everyday life (neighboring repetition) might be compared to the carnival game in which, one at a time and at seemingly arbitrary and certainly unpredictable moments and places, targets pop into view and then drop back out of sight, though not so fast that one can't take a shot at them. The trivialization and debunking of the ordinary and everyday is a product of the aftershock of "make it new." Between Ashby and Russell, walking north and all but imperceptibly uphill along the east side of College Avenue, one first passes the Elmwood branch of the WELLS FARGO BANK, then BOSS ROBOT (a tiny model and toy shop, specializing in remote control toys and mechanical toys from Japan), then a storefront under renovation (formerly ELMWOOD HARDWARE), ELMWOOD STATIONERS, THE GEM GALLERY (a jewelry store), BILL'S TRADING POST (specializing in Native American jewelry and artifacts), LA TOUR (a hair salon), ELEMENTS (a clothing shop), TREEHOUSE (another gift shop), THE BEANERY (a coffee shop and bakery), SWEET DREAMS (a toy store), LA FOOT (a shoe store, specializing in athletic shoes), VILLAGE SHOES (a shoe store), BODY TIME (a knock-off of THE BODY SHOP, selling soaps, ointments, bath supplies, hair clips, etc.); COTTON BASICS (a clothing shop), A.G. FERRARA (an Italian delicatessen), SONAM (a Tibetan gift shop), IT'S PARTY TIME (a party supply shop, replacing TEDDY'S LITTLE CLOSET, a children's clothing shop), and finally SWEET DREAMS (a candy shop, affiliated with the toy store down the street). Everyone is anticipating fireworks later, willing the fog to dissipate. The children in the plaza are hastily putting their shoes back on, shouting out plans, giddy with eagerness, afraid of getting left behind. The approaching Marching Homeland Band is unimaginably vast, with its 500 drummers and what are rumored to be several thousand trumpeters along with frightening phalanxes of men and women with trombones whose slides they thrust and pull and thrust again upward like golden sabers or scythes, and it is coming over the horizon toward us, crushing the yellow grass and future melons and playgrounds. "These details, which are incorrectly termed little ——— there being neither little facts in humanity nor little leaves in vegetation ——— are useful," as Victor Hugo says. In this context, dreaming is an act of disreputable profundity. In response to criticism (that it's useless, a waste of money, etc.), the managers of NASA's Mars Phoenix mission, which is exploring a polar region of Mars in search of vestigial evidence of once-existing life, have replied that the mission's true purpose is to find us "a new home." Despite the "economic downturn," there has been a huge increase in the numbers of tourists in San Francisco, and in the amount of money they are spending: 16 million visitors were here last year, and they spent $8.2 billion (a 6.2% increase over the year before). And more and more U.S. soldiers are committing suicide. Victor Hugo and Leo Tolstoy were writing their respective epics (Les Misérables and War and Peace) at more or less the same time. It took Victor Hugo fifteen years to write Les Misérables. He began it in 1845 but three years later his work was interrupted by politics (the uprising of 1848, in which he participated; the short-lived Second Republic; his opposition to Napoleon III and the coup d'état that brought him to power; his subsequent flight and exile in Guernsey). He finished the book in 1860 and then went back and added to it. Les Misérables was published in 1862. An initial draft of War and Peace was published in 1863 (though Tolstoy then went back and rewrote the work, which came out in its final version in 1869). War and Peace covers an eight-year span, from 1805 to 1813 in Russia; Les Misérables covers the approximately twenty-year long period in France beginning just after the Napoleonic Wars and Napoleon's exile. Hugo, in other words, shows us France in the wake of the defeat it has suffered in the Russia of Tolstoy's novel. "What would art be, as the writing of history, if it shook off the memory of accumulated suffering?" Adorno asks (at the end of Aesthetic Theory). For the mouth neither death nor candy nor lumber from felled trees used to frame the windows set in the walls through which one crawls into the artists' quarter of a city and hence into the future that belongs to the students or to the pigeons that politicize them; death, candy, and lumber belong to the emperors of global capitalism. Adorno remarks that "art reaches toward reality, only to recoil at the actual touch of it" (It is equally plausible to claim that art delights in reaching reality; it depends on the nature of that "reality," on whether it is the site of the catastrophe of human history that Adorno, with justification, thinks it to be or whether it is, rather, an unjudged simple suchness (of, say, today's beautiful weather, the red chair in which I'm sitting, the ambient household sounds, etc.)). Art reaches toward an ontological reality and encounters historical reality ——— perhaps this is why it recoils. Looking for my dark glasses, I find several left around the room, and I try them, one by one, but each in turn blurs the things around me until I put on a pair through which I can see fine. I look around: here are various spoons, bowls, a four-burner gas stove, etc., and a window, this one unfortunately looking out over a narrow alley onto the façade of the building next door and into the neighbors' kitchen. A spark falls to the floor and burns a hole clear through it. I catch a glimpse of a microcephalic cow, and then, apparently kept in the same pen, a turkey-headed pig steps into view. The imagination has, in Walter Benjamin's words, "remarkable propensity for structures that convey and connect." For the writer of everyday life, even to the extent that she deploys some of the strategies of the diarist, memory comes into play (though it takes various, sometimes minor as well as major, roles). But, even if she doesn't record things at the precise moment they occur but only does so later, her chronicle will be configured, rather than, in the conventional sense, plotted. Or rather, it is plotted but as land or a map is, with elements placed here and there. The resulting paratactically configured work keeps first her and then our attention on immediate particulars in the present tense, since that is the tense of cognitive time. It is the temporality, too, by the way, of encounters with the dictionary, since almost no one moves through a dictionary from front to back. What would an alphabetical ordering of the sentences in the paragraph preceding this one look like? But a digression inserted at this point would be less entertaining than irritating, though of course the author may intend to irritate, why should she feel bound to entertain? A digression would produce something like the situation of the three young peasant soldiers, a woman and two men, who are making their way into enemy territory: someone shouts "your fly" or "the fly," referring to a missing insignia on the woman's jacket, and afraid of being exposed (afraid that they've already been spotted), the three young soldiers disappear into a crowd of people swarming into a department store. For an instant the sunlight coming through the open window picks up a stain or shadow on the floor so pale and transient I'm not sure what I'm seeing, and in just that way a memory is haunted by doubt and an event by a fly.

15

A young woman roars, laughs, splashes the face of a young man, nears the shore where the blinking lights of fireflies flash under the trees, gets pregnant, and thereafter, from the corner of her eye, she watches her every step as if expecting to see a different sun set every evening into the impressions they leave as she goes about her days. "Twilight was beginning to whiten everything above and blacken everything below." So Victor Hugo describes the end of a 19th-century day on the rural outskirts of Paris. Evening arrives again, thirty-five pages later: "A few constellations here and there in the deep pale heavens, the earth all black, the sky all white, a shivering in the blades of grass, everywhere the mysterious thrill of twilight." The pregnant woman's attention drifts to the side, as if looking to the peripheries, to glimpse something indirectly and aside, and there to discover, amid myriad details, configurations that reveal things no one else knows, or that everyone else chooses not to notice. But the operative position for a logical conclusion is not at the end of elements in a sequence but between them. Typical empirical logic, temporally bound as it is to the chronologic of cause-and-effect, assumes that, from a little sequence of two occurrences, one following the other, a connection between them can be made.

> A: The soldiers fire their rifles.
> B: Rosalinda falls to the floor.
> C: Conclusion: The soldiers have shot Rosalinda.

With element C we establish a connection: A, C, therefore B. The events ——— the interventions ——— that contribute to a particular plot (and to the larger landscapes that it lays out) are registered as temporal in various senses ——— as historical, as grammatical, as generational, as cyclical, as chronic. Daily activities and agricultural seasons stir eddies over the terrain. The present activities that we undertake habitually are thick with past. It is a past whose presence is logical (what sufficed yesterday should suffice today; what worked yesterday should work today), but it is also, especially to the degree that it is automatic, not only arbitrary but preconditional. As Barbara Maria Stafford says, "Living in a society means learning, largely automatically, to repeat forms of behavior that already existed." These "forms of behavior" are empty forms ——— "arbitrary" ——— until they are filled with today's behavior. "The only way to remember a place for ever is to live in the place for an hour; and the only way to live in the place for an hour is to forget the place for an hour. The undying scenes we can all see if we shut our eyes are not the scenes that we have stared at under the direction of guide-books; the scenes we see are the scenes at which we did not look at all ——— the scenes in which we walked when we were thinking about something else [...]. We can see the background now because we did not see it then." In the distant past humans were energized by their delusions, and yet we relentlessly sought to rid ourselves of them. Perhaps this is why people are so fond of having feelings when they recognize each other. "Don't go for the obvious," Askari Nate Martin tells the kids of the OAKLAND MAP as he sends them out for the morning with cameras or sketchpads, fifteen of them, age 12 to 16. "Are we looking for clues to existence?" asks Tamarind Magee. In her right ear lobe she's wearing a paper clip, she has elevated it to the status of jewelry. Tamarind doesn't like to waste a minute. She's playing with Askari Nate Martin, with his having been a cop and having quit "the copping," as QJ puts it. Time is almost always experienced peripherally. It appears only in effects. Time is a stylist or a killer. Whatever it is transacting, it is over there somewhere, or behind us, we may have missed it. Maybe we each have an eye at the back of our head, though we haven't yet thought, or dared, to open it. There are people who believe this to be true of everyone. Or maybe the eye was open and now we're blinking, but the blink takes a human lifetime. When we blink we moisten our eyes, but that's not the reason for the blinking. We blink to give our brain a break, a moment of respite from the influx of information. Or, rather, we give it a chance to make sense of what it has seen. "People's motives are completely opaque to me," says Maxine

Able Smith to Dorothy Blythe Ward. "I understand agency but not causation." To the left of the sandwich shop on the plaza the group of teenagers mills around each other. One darts away and darts back, laughing, another shouts. A second suddenly thrusts his open plastic water bottle in the direction of the first, splashing her. A third splashes a fourth. The teenagers charge, splash, leap back, shriek, hoot, demonstrating joyously or perhaps in utter anxiety and wishfulness their collectivity, their belonging to their group. Maggie Fornetti and Dewanda Horn cross the plaza, watching the kids askance. Nothing is happening; nothing is always happening. Those kids are fighting for visibility, Dewanda says. They've got their theme, says Maggie. They are only haphazardly notable. In this place, they are never simple, never quotidian, says Dewanda; they're excessive. But not as expensive as they'd be in prison, says Maggie Fornetti. In order to perceive something, one has to believe something about it, consciously or ———— more likely ———— not. History does not provide literature with smooth transitions. It's a Wednesday afternoon, 3:45 pm, in late July. Francesca Malaya Martin is in a window seat near the back of the #51B bus, her backpack on her lap. To escape ———— or at least loosen ———— the strictures of the middle class takes time. It takes linear time, the kind of time the Enlightenment made primary and perhaps even mandatory, time for <u>progress</u>. Francesca Malaya Martin is considering a paradox: she has to make progress against progress. This is not too subtle a project; she does not consider herself apart from whatever interests her at the moment. The bus crosses Russell Street, moving slowly. On the right, ornate gold lettering on the closed glass door of the store that used to be LORA'S CLOSET now spells out GOORIN'S HAT SHOP. A man in a wheelchair with a dog is trying to maneuver past people waiting their turn to enter ICI. He tugs on the dog's leash to pull it closer to the wheelchair as people in the crowd, only half-consciously noticing him, nonetheless move just enough to let him pass. We only sometimes organize things according to their alphabetical aspect ————A for apple, anadiplosis, accident, and C for click, creek, and cheese, C for ceaseless combining and citizenship, C for cities, chrysanthemum, for cave paintings, which is what Malaya and Maggie had been talking about over breakfast. To appreciate something's beauty, and even more its matter-of-factness, one must enter the environment as a part of it. Rhythms of cognition are set by attention and mutated by participation, improvised, in time. Making sense is an adventure of the moment. This is as true for Francesca Malaya Martin at age 12 as it is for me in my 70s. Time is invisible, uncaused, and within it we can experience absolute freedom. But history, of course, curtails it. During the period of Language Writing's emergence, various historians (as, for example, the Annales group, with volumes by Fernand Braudel and Lucien Febvre just coming out in English) and cultural anthropologists (particularly Clifford Geertz) were practicing what's been termed a "turn to ordinariness" and producing "thick descriptions." Might Ron Silliman's Ketjak or my My Life represent turns to the ordinary, might they be said to favor thick descriptions, offering accounts of what E.P. Thompson termed "history from below"? Francesca Malaya Martin gets off the bus at the corner of Woolsey and College, walks one block west on Woolsey, and then turns south on Benvenue. The late afternoon sun is warm on her shoulders, her shadow jumps forward as it meets a wall, undulates over the fissures, bulges, concavities, and niches of the sidewalk. They undergo her shadow. There are figures in them, things that, like the Pleiades, can only be seen peripherally. They are a distinguishable though indistinct sphere of reality, emergent rather than clear. Perhaps what Language Writing was making was not a "turn to ordinariness" as it was understood by Thompson and others, a turn away from history as the record of heroes and great deeds. Rather, it was making a turn to difference ——— thus to language itself, certainly, but also to that which resists it, the unidentifiable in social and narrative terrains: undomesticated women, for instance, or narratives that won't let you in or haven't let you out. The conditions of failure, in other words. The moment of difference is the moment that writing can't write, projected into the future even as it is preserved in nostalgia, experienced in pathos, and expressed by gaps in logic, rationality, understanding. Francesca passes the neighbor's old white dog lolling on a patch of grass and pauses. Jonah Martin is sitting on the front steps of their house, concentrating on a Nintendo/DS game in his hands. The con- nection between them, C, might be temporal ———contingency. In the distance, but not a great distance, someone is just pull- ing a nail, and farther away a dog barks. Time is noisy. Shrimp click, caterpillars munch, and two students on mopeds clatter through the neighborhood. The painter Jean Millet is said to have once remarked that trees are like people who don't speak one's language. If one could abandon one's penchant for self-scrutiny, itself both the gift and curse of the bourgeois individualist's sensitivity, one might see others ——— the oth- ers. But where would one start?

16

In the early evening before dinner, a child I will call A becomes a dog. The process takes approximately ten minutes and culminates in the bestowing ——— the self-bestowing ——— of a name: uttering the last bit of human speech the child will use for an hour, A says, "I am Jujube." Jujube is a melodramatic figure playing the central role in a theater of becoming-adult whose predominant theme is lost love. Jujube is kenneled in a world of strangers and yearning for release, which she identifies with moving forward on a leash. She sticks out her tongue and seizes a length of heavy string draped over a chair; she pulls it into her mouth and shakes it. The leash will be the measure of her attachments, with it she will tug the world. Amplitude has to be pulled close. It is with an assertion of hope that a vast and diverse new field of interdisciplinary experimentation, critique, and aesthetic expansion has emerged. Carla Harryman writes: "Hope, or utopian desire, is a kind of engine of our qualitative life that drives us forward with a sense not that miraculously there will be a change for the better but rather that one is a participant in change and that one can participate in inspiring change; even works of art that seem to enlist or project forms of negativity can be signs or symptoms of hopeful thought and desire." Social play has the potential to produce a workable version of solidarity. There should be an ontological, animal sufficiency to its moment, a working pause. Thereafter, whether it's the continuities or the discontinuities that will prevail will remain to be seen. Which will have greater explanatory power? Greater sustaining power? Which will offer the better opportunities for justice, understanding, happiness? "What you are able to construct in language," Fredric Jameson notes, "has a certain truth by virtue of that very wresting of language, not merely from silence as such, but from the baleful properties of the proposition form, the perils of thematization and reification, and the inevitable (and metaphysical) illusions and distortions of the requirement to begin and end at certain points, and to appeal to this or that conventional standard of argument and of evidence." It's 6:30 pm, someone on a skateboard goes by, the rhythmic rumble and clack (as the board rides over a crack) fade as Maggie Fornetti adds a half-cup of chicken broth to the risotto and absent-mindedly stirs it. We have to be able to imagine Anna Karenina or Pierre Bezukhov living their everyday lives. Anna chooses a pair of gloves, is restless. She removes the gloves and touches her throat with the fingers of her right hand. She lets her fingers slip down the surface of her blouse, as if inadvertently, and across the nipple of her left breast. She sighs and is uncomfortable ———— Tolstoy suggests as much. Pierre slips on his boots. He can still taste the pickled cabbage that was served with his soup, though Tolstoy doesn't say so. Realism lies not in such details but in the knowledge that they exist. Actuality is even more complicated. "Actuality" is the term Kierkegaard in <u>Either/Or</u> prefers to "reality." The latter for Kierkegaard implies conformance with "truth," the latter connotes coming into being in a specific time and place. "What I've got is not knowledge but difference," says Askari Nate Martin. "Then me, too," says Jonah Giacomo Martin. "He who can't learn new tricks is an old dog," says Carmen Kandia Martin, breezily. "Listen to my story," says Jonah: "Something stirred on a cold night," he reads; "That's the hook," he says. "Cody jumped when he finished making dinner. He went to the lake the next day and he found a very dark and gloomy cave. Apparently Cody was adventurous. He went into the cave and he saw a shape in a shadow. Then a monstrous wingéd creature flew over him and he fell backward into the cave, but he was fine." The multiple speakers of, say, English, or ———— to limit our sample ———— speakers for whom American English is their first (and perhaps only) language, do not necessarily share a single world view, except in the most general sense. It is not American English so much as the language culture of English-speaking America that inculcates in its citizens certain expectations and assumptions, as well as certain anxieties and proclivities. From its own sphere, the money culture does much the same. One way or another, every citizen stands in relation to the flow of exchange through which society is deemed to exist. The good citizen is expected to produce and sell and profit and buy; perhaps he or she hopes, too, to profit and rise —— beyond judgment, perhaps, without breaking stride. Here are twelve figures in the once current or prospective flow of exchange —— a jury of sorts. There are six men and six women (we will begin equitably if not necessarily justly). I myself refuse to play the part of "judge." A proposition, like a description, or a fiction, is only a small theory, not a judgment. Just as the opinions of a thoughtful person can leap from doubt to doubt and waver at the edge of decision, so I will try to imagine a dozen perspectives, inhabit a dozen contexts, devise a dozen means for forming an opinion or coming to a decision. I am Samuel Wang Xie, 51 years old, notary public and owner of a small documents business providing passport photos, ID photos, fingerprinting scans, shredding services. I am Marisa Emily Wetherington, 29, a public health nurse, with no children and in the midst of an acrimonious divorce for which I consider myself largely to blame. I am Alejandro Javier Rodriguez, 39 years old, the divisional head of IT for the Department of Motor Vehicles. I am Lyn Hejinian, writing this on a summer day without quite knowing who's on trial or what kinds of accusation are in play. I am Michael Montane Afewerek, 47 years old or thereabouts, owner of ETHIOPIQUITY, a music club and café. I am Julie Claire Baine, 65 years old, former vice-president of the Western States Bingo Association, now retired. I am Billy Frederick Johnson, age 49, landscape arborist for the city's public works department. I am Stanley Demand Dennis, age 54, a butcher for SAFEWAY. I am Maria Ana Sanchez-Fried, age 32, ninth-grade math teacher at Sojourner Truth Middle School. I am Hoa Mia Macintyre, age 22, city college student. I am Gabriel Espinosa, age 24, I've been looking for a job for months, now I'm thinking about joining the army. I am Milly Margaret Willis, age 56, child welfare attorney.

> I am omnipresent to some extent,
> but how should I direct my attention
>
> sufficiently to what I desire, to
> stop, to
> what is charging on the roadbed, what

                    going away, the
            fire-gong, people and buses

                and even in my room, as
        I know
                    the waving sun
                                the
        constant ephemerals

Some of these ——— Larry Eigner's ephemerals (I am quoting
from a poem of his), my figures ——— I would like to befriend,
I want their approval. But Samuel Wang Xie, Marisa Emily
Wetherington, Lyn Hejinian, and the others ——— they are all
figments of my imagination. "B" (though perhaps more clearly
in sections of the poem that I'm not quoting) would seem to
be a poem about history, or about a sequence of "moments"
experienced as historical rather than as gifts to a bourgeois sen-
sorium. Eigner's aesthetic sensibility resists the leveling tides of
history and the anonymity, the immateriality, they leave in their
wake. Every actuality gets lost. Prior to that, every actuality gets
found, or made. Eigner's poem captions recovered, or imagined,
fragments of lost reality. But nowhere does he emblematize it,
or himself, as a site of loss. The bond (which was only an appar-
ent one) between language and reality, sign and signified, can
no longer be assumed. But this doesn't end their relevance to
each other, which is not solely ironic. Here, on the other hand,
is an ironic poem on precisely that theme ——— the linguistic
detachment of meaning from occasion and experience:

        tive mate rect ward cal nipresent solutely
        sition etic ment berg ner nomenon torious tinually
        dition ualities etically mains its tuality one ification
        tened man ing ality's come siasm tic
                cisely preted ful tory jected
                tic ity sence trolled ny's ing

The poem's aesthetic appeal is limited. It's rhythmic, but not
fully musical. Conclusions are with us, but their contexts seem to
have been jettisoned. Juries are convened, criteria are provided,

they are made to understand what they have been summoned
to decide, but all grounds for effecting change are withheld.
The great Joyce scholar David Hayman, writing about the prom-
inence of judicial motifs in Finnegans Wake, suggests "that the
paternalistic control imposed by legal systems is strictly a day-
time or solar phenomenon and that in the timeless/spaceless
universe of the unconscious, of the instinctual, or the Mothers,
it can only be a shadow presence." Is it obsessiveness, then, or
superstition that drives me to step out the front door with my
right foot first on odd-numbered days and my left foot first on
even? What's at stake isn't luck but justice; I am committed
to giving my feet equal though alternating priority, they take
turns being in first place. I'm fully aware of the absurdity of
this, and the level of satisfaction produced by my attending to
my feet equally is far from great. Nonetheless, my proprioce-
tive senses, although admittedly only half-conscious, get tuned
to the surroundings. I enter into the ambient sounds and famil-
iar sights of the neighborhood, and, at least for a moment, all
seems right. This moment of satisfaction, active and physio-
logical, has the energy of a small theory, it forms an attitude
with which I identify: "'so be it': the ultimate expression of will
aligned with what the world makes available." Then desire and
dissonance (whether in the form of indifference, disassocia-
tion, or distance) are not mutually exclusive. One's everyday life
(dormant repetition) is like one's shadow, binding one to the
ground, elongated early and late in the day and directly under
one's feet at noon. So we can talk about the "hidden meaning"
of a poem. Just as it is dreaming rather than the so-called latent
(or repressed) content of a dream that harbors the dream's real
mystery, and just as it is the social relations of production rather
than the commodity they produce that remains in thrall to cap-
italism, so it is that the relationships and interactions of all the
elements of a work of art hold its meaning. The hidden meaning
of a poem, in other words, resides in and as its plot, which is not
a matter of what Ato Quayson terms "inexorable sequentiality"
but of the totality of all the elements at play in the work ———
its diverse discursive levels, changing modes, complementary
devices, contradictory motifs, etc., along with all the epistemo-
logical and affective realms pertinent to them. The work of art

offers an experience of contradictions and incommensurabili-
ties ———— these are much better than truths. Poetry has drawn
its capacity for criticism into itself. Contradictory feelings pre-
vail. Elements of a story appear, but it's a story punctuated with
numerous gaps; these serve as perfect hiding places. Periodically,
as the story develops, predictions are made: about a pair of lov-
ers, the value of real estate, or an impending rhyme, and they
turn out to be more or less accurate or inaccurate. A conver-
sation begins, identities circulate, attaching to one statement,
then another. Carmen Kandia Martin feels sassy. "My life," says
Askari Nate Martin, "is continuous with the historical world, but
not with the neighborhood I live in." Either everyday life (intu-
ited repetition) is a site of utter conformity into which we are
completely assimilated or it's a site of subversion and resis-
tance. "I defy anyone to project my life onto these streets,"
says Nate, "and, especially, into those backyards," he waves
toward the kitchen window. "Grandpa," says Malaya, "says life
isn't about happiness." "Grandma," Jonah says, "says it is." "I
can't use their categories," says Nate, and Carmen says he'd be
better off if he tried. One's responses to aesthetic experience
are bound to one's affective values ———— to the feelings one
aspires to keep available to the manner in which one lives one's
life. The aesthetic obsessions are emotional. In a world whose
enchantments are irrelevant (in which a story's cold night is only
a "hook"), they can seem irrational, or at least illogical; greed,
cruelty, and even stupidity are more relevant than the desires
that the aesthetic provokes or, sometimes, satisfies. Let the
aesthetic, then, be relegated to the quotidian world, the ubiqui-
tous sphere of everyday life. There it can generate vividness and
intensities. A in the guise of Jujube is taking on the problem of
language. She's purporting to be conversant with the vocal and
postural signifying system of a dog. She cringes, fawns, whines,
lifts a paw, waggles her butt, barks. And I? I take on the sig-
nificance of the delighted, prescient, attentive new owner of
a puppy, but I find it taxing, I can't sustain it. I put a handful of
Cheerios into a bowl and put it on the floor. A/Jujube thrusts
her face into the bowl. Maggie Fornetti checks the risotto, puts
a dollop of crème fraîche on each of six small salmon fillets and
slides them into the oven, and removes six artichokes from the

two pots in which they've been steaming. Maggie Fornetti gives the larger pot ———— her favorite ———— a quick rub for good luck. There are analogies to be found between the structure of <u>The Arabian Nights</u>, with its stories within stories, the structure of the psyche in Freud's account of it, with its co-existing conscious and unconscious mental lives whose "systems are pictured as relatively autonomous persons-within-the-person," and the structure of the urban everyday, with its interrelated but independent and autonomous moments and events circulating through the moments and events of others. In the fiction whose figures include Askari Nate Martin, Maggie Fornetti, and their three children, A is Antonia Alice Martin, age 6, currently Jujube. Her twelve-year old sister Francesca Malaya Martin enters the Jujube game and takes Antonia out of the kitchen on the leash. Everyday life requires artistry. The quotidian harbors aesthetic effects and can offer aesthetic experiences, but, lodged as they are in the everyday, they are hard to evaluate. But every art form invites participation in its own way. Attending the ballet, for example, caught up in the sheer impossibility (in the artifice and athleticism) of the medium, psycho-somatically, sitting still in my seat, I dance. With this naïve, virtual mimesis, wherein I lose my subjective difference from the objective dance, I partake intensely of aesthetic enjoyment. It is not the entirety of the experience (or experiencing) of the ballet, however; I also remain at a rational distance from the dancers and review the dance as a cartographer or field botanist might, and this is the negative substance of the experience, which keeps me from dancing and dancing from me. That negativity is not the negativity of condemnation, nor dislike, nor any other pejorative feeling or judgment. It is simply the negativity that informs and is essential to the knowledge expressed by such statements as "this is not that" or, as in this case, "I am not dancing"; it establishes and maintains the alterity that, in turn, makes the ballet, for example, so strangely compelling. Later I find myself engulfed in an excess of reason ———— natural and unnatural reasons, reasons in conflict. In a world of limitless sun, it is logical that there would be a superfluity of reason.

17

A writer, a Latina poet (this is how she describes herself) has written (to me, though not with particular personal animosity) to express her rage at "post-avant" writers' theft of the "border," which they have appropriated and turned into a concept and a trope. A battlefield, a kitchen, a city street, a bed, a subway car: any of these might be a site where humans gather. We dis, de, con, sub, pre, co, un, sur, ex, and pro. All that's determined can be distermined too. The tongue in love will play and play, ante and fore, circum, re, and retro. There are few predators that will kill a sleeping beast —————— the dog in its slumber, the napping cat, the bird with its head hidden under its wing. I dream of foodstuffs —————— that's the word: little containers —————— caviar in jars, yogurt in plastic cups, plastic-wrapped half-sandwiches or quarter-sandwiches in styrofoam trays —————— I have snack-paks —————— but security wouldn't let any of it through, everything is confiscated, and I find myself with an empty, sky-blue canvas satchel, cleared to travel. No appointments, no errands scheduled. My plan? It is Askari Nate Martin, not I, who, incapable himself of betrayal, can't imagine being betrayed. But daily life and art occupy different space-times; a museum, a concert hall, a page of text, an art gallery are more likely to be experienced as refuges from daily life than as its venue. The object of all this is that on which sunlight is cast: the day. And more than that. There's a somewhat outdated world globe standing on a table not far from me. Since it was made, certain national borders have shifted, some nations have come into existence, disappeared, or been renamed. But many features have remained the same. The morning sun, reflected off a window pane, is visible on the surface of the Philippine Sea, an iridescent circle all but obliterating the Marianas. This is no mere contradiction. One's banal, quotidian exchanges with grocery clerks, postal clerks, strangers in waiting lines, etc. are manifestations of a certain degree of sociability, acknowledgement, friendliness, but also and above all curiosity; one engages with people one hardly knows or doesn't know at all in order to find out about them. When one says "Amazing weather, isn't it?" it should be translated as "Who are you?" The clichéd observation that "you can't take it with you" applies not only to money but to the contents of the inner life in which one keeps one's hoard of memories and impressions, the treasure house (or is it a prison house?) so dear to the artist and intellectual as to the bourgeoisie. Were the sun able to see everyday life to its depths, it might think heretically, with us. "Through violations of the orthodoxy of thought, something in the object becomes visible which it is orthodoxy's secret and objective aim to keep invisible." It is not thoughts themselves that contain artistry but the way they are assembled. That is what's human here: the way in which the thoughts (ideas, observations, described sensations and emotions, perceptions, etc.) are held. Are you following all this, self and other? Or is it addressing only the other, a pair of thoughtless eyes? Has the self gone off? Xavier de Maistre, perhaps unduly influenced by Descartes (though alive in different centuries, they were both French, after all), knows something of this useless situation. "When you read a book, sir [or madam], and a more agreeable [or more compelling] idea suddenly strikes on your imagination, your soul straight away pounces on it and forgets the book, while your eyes mechanically follow the words and the lines; you come to the end of the page [or paragraph] without understanding it, and without remembering what you have read. ——— This comes from the fact that your soul, having ordered its companion to read to it, did not warn it of the brief absence on which it was about to embark; as a result, the other continued to read even though your soul was no longer listening." To transit a great work of music, art, history, mathematics, philosophy, or literature, the good listener, viewer, or reader rides in a supernatural cart. The cart has the ability, while advancing, not to advance. In front of the cart is a pair of horses, named either Push and Pull or To and Fro. The heroine, a factory worker and now an old woman, at the end of the Polish film Strike reflects on what has happened: "It was a great victory back then and we didn't realize that the strike would change all of Europe. We didn't think that in six years, the Berlin Wall would fall and Poland would be a free country again. And we didn't know that by winning, we would lose what we had been fighting for. Our solidarity. Being divided, we couldn't undo all harm and injustice. It is now up to the next generations to deal with it." Or fictional characters —————— they are often found in confrontations with history. But Maggie Fornetti doesn't understand Askari Nate Martin, nor does his friend Constantine Donegan. "Is it a black thing, your self-containment?" Maggie asks. Nate often radiates resistance, she thinks, or an indifference that has the same alienating effect. Maggie's abundance of character makes her impossible to negate, but she is frequently disappointed, and actively so, which is to say that she is often angry. When she isn't, the joy she experiences is extreme. What does it mean to "take it on faith" that one is loved by one's beloved? What has the beloved asked of one, what has he assumed, when he makes it clear that his love is to be taken on faith? "Maybe you're overlooking things," says Dewanda Horn. Perpetually and by its nature caught up in the present, the paratactic work is devoid of fate until the very last moment of its existence, when everything in it has taken its place, when it is itself a totality and thus also a particular. The long and tangled sequence becomes an infinite consequence. Just to set out to write numerous impressions of the day for a week would keep one watching like a subversive or saboteur for opportune moments produced by the day. Some small birds, which might have been juncos and were almost chickadees appeared when the wind subsided that had earlier been bending the tops of trees westward only to release and then bend them again. "I pity you, unhappy stars [...], for you do not love," says Goethe in his "Night Thoughts." To which is advertising closest —————— comedy or pathos? I read an ad, written in large black type on a white billboard, offering people a quart of paint for use on a nearby fence; the quart will last for up to 2 hours of painting. The price for the paint and the time with it is first listed as $1, then as "one bloom." I want to do it: "life, extended through art." Homo sapiens emerged as a distinct hominid species around 150,000 years ago in Africa and soon began to spread out, reaching Europe around 110,000 years later. Though the dating is still disputed, it appears that it took us another 25,000 years to establish ourselves on the

North American continent. "The increase of men meant the deepening of shadow." That observation, when it was made, referred to crowds. Simultaneity is a phenomenon produced in interpretation, it's not inherent to occurrence itself. Coincidence is generated through observation, and marks something as an occasion rather than merely an occurrence. It weds our notions of fortune or fate to those of event or history. Stephen Spielberg's film "Jurassic Park" is in some ways a reworking of Eliot's "The Waste Land," but Spielberg makes a significant change, adding children to the landscape who can bear witness not only to the violence and destruction but also to the physical and mental clumsiness of the adult humans whose misguided experimentation bring it about. "The great god Pan is dead" according to a Greek authority of 2000 years ago. The death coincided with Christ's birth ——— a disastrous substitution. I continue to hear ghosts in the voice of an august consternation. This is the tale called Fortune's Dispute with Luck. Four yellow pencils lie on the desk, in mourning. An inexorable trapezoid of sunlight is approaching and behind it slides the hard metallic shadow of the window frame. The sunlight is an inevitability, a velocity, a plight. The beeping of a backing delivery truck drives its counterpoint into the shifting shadows floating on the pavement under the ruthless sweet pittosporum tree. The sun, deliquescent, sinks. By bringing into her work entirely unfamiliar (although English) words (which she found by browsing in a dictionary), Leslie Scalapino hoped, she said, to create a world that had been unknown to her, a world with a future, a hitherto unknown possibility. A long, low wooden boat, which is painted white and a tranquil, pale slate-blue, swings into a swift but not turbulent current of clear water, and, hardly bobbing, we drift with it. A beach, basking in the peripheries, appears on the right, and we come to rest in an eddy against what is now a brittle embankment. We have achieved not an eternal moment but eternal movement. What starts out as a simple "to do" list on one's computer turns into an obsessive diary never able to record everything that takes place between "Woke" and "Then to sleep." The sun is 149.6 million kilometers (93 million miles) away. I can't help overhearing fragments of a tale that a somewhat exasperated, somewhat tremulous diminutive man is recounting to a bank teller through the thick, bulletproof glass. From what I can understand, he has spent the previous few weeks helping his mother move into a retirement home. She's given him "50 crystal ——— I said <u>crystal</u> ——— wine glasses, and I don't even drink," he says fervently ——— avidly ——— desperately ——— as if afraid. There's no point. Might just as well straighten one's teeth. I don't think the teller can hear him. His and her routines are embedded in a sonic panorama: a passing bus, a shrieking infant, wind in the trees, the whine of an electric saw, a passing mechanical street sweeper, the bark of a dog. And under us the earth is filled with gold, which grows like carrots, which is carried to the surface by ants, which is mined by naked boys who live in holes. Habit makes its appearance disguised as spontaneity. The foregrounding of details needn't mean that the background, for all that, is secondary. Both Leo Tolstoy, in the descriptions of battle he includes in <u>War and Peace</u>, and Victor Hugo, in the battle (at Waterloo) that he puts into <u>Les Misérables</u>, speak of the obliterating smoke, a kind of battle fog, that rising off the field makes what's happening unclear. At the end of the day, the sun, which has been "fighting to break through," withdraws, like the source of an idea. What idea? The idea that inspired Hugo's long description of the Battle of Waterloo? It is an idea about tyranny and temporality and history and destiny and the deceptiveness of the lay of the land. I should mention arrogance, too ——— the self-deceptive arrogance of declining power ——— and then there's contingency. In the supermarket the lights over the tiered products flicker, the senses are excited, the pyramided tomatoes are laid out as if in preparation for play.

18

How does a writer, or a serious artist of any kind, make it possible for someone to understand, and then to care about, what he or she is doing? It isn't out of arrogance that the avant-garde writer doesn't linger very long over the problem (if there is one) of accessibility implicit in such a question. One key goal of the historical avant-garde was to assert the primacy of art's autonomy, from which would extend its authority and its self-evident right to significance. Inherent to the realization of that goal was resistance to external influences. "In the case of the avant-garde, it is an argument of self-assertion or self-defense used by a society in the strict sense against society in the larger sense," as Renato Poggioli says in his seminal study, The Theory of the Avant-Garde. "No, Fred," Poggioli said. Sibyls prophesy, but so inefficiently (so unintelligibly) as to preclude the possibility that they do so with the intention of making beneficial interventions, of providing practical help. Their prophetic utterances have no utilitarian value. The status of their utterances is aesthetic, their effect spiritual. One on gustily drilling F to D bark but then and flick-off if. Fuck-out off. One over. Rosa-Jane Stein is on the name grid ——— Russell Baldwin Wright inhales to digress. You know why ——— don't you? You are getting the ideas, the worldview, an accurate sense of the stakes involved here, the purport of the language ——— aren't you? Am I? What schemes bind accessibilities together, what tapes keep sites off-limits, and what are those sites, seemingly so distinct from what's accessible? We know of a person sleeping that he or she is alive but we wouldn't say, as he or she sleeps, that he or she is living his or her life. Aesthetic rapture is different from erotic rapture in that one doesn't want to lose oneself in, or become the object of, the former; on the contrary, one wants to stand apart from it, precisely so as to enjoy oneself and others aesthetically (rather than, say, procreatively). Sunlight falls on a leafy street tree and I'm elated by the pattern of shadows it casts on the wall of the ugly apartment building with the blinding façade that neighbors the house in which I wander, work, brush my teeth, cook, wash, sleep. If I were to film, as I'd very much like to, those shadows as they intersect, separate, intensify, shiver, I would do so so that you could see them, too. If one can't show others what one sees, tell others what one knows, it's as if one is the only person awake in a world of sleepers. Avant-garde art is an art of shared wakefulness (and perhaps an art of insomniacs). To ask how or why something exists or happens already assumes that it exists or happens. There's to be a neighborhood street party, the street will be blocked off from noon to 10 pm, there will be games for the children, music, food. The party is underway. But wait ——— we need more preparation, more room, more beauty. We don't want a featureless sky, and the ugly apartment building with its blind façade should disappear. Negative space is a medium of continuity. But just how rational ——— how intricately argued, how logical ——— is this? The diverse elements in the paragraphs go about their business reasonably enough, the syntax and vocabulary are generally that of rationalist discourse, figures step out from the background now and then, and the ground itself (the underground) is solid enough. But a distinction needs to be made, here, between the uninterpretability of the concrete particular ——— what George Oppen called the "mineral fact," a rock or cat, say, whose quiddity we can assert ("there it is") but whose quality we can't query ——— and the resistant tactics of avant-garde writing. I can identify with a character I'll call Tamarind Magee, and this isn't only, or even significantly, because I made her up ——— am making her up. Tamarind Magee is a version of myself, not as I was but as I might have been if I'd been an unhappy child as well as a willful one. I made up Askari Nate Martin, too, and Maggie Fornetti, and Leo X. Lee, but not Charlie Altieri or Jean Day, both of whom are real people, bound to their own individual nexus of identifications, stirred by different particulars. Nonetheless, Jean Day and I have together participated in many protest actions together, including an afternoon blockade of the main entrance to a bank on a warm Tuesday just after Labor Day. It is hard to say when this protest began ——— years ago, or at noon, or half an hour before that, when Jean and I met as planned at the union office to pick up some placards, or in the cycle of frustration, political grief, anger, excitement, optimism, and determination that are continuous with my venturing forth everyday from the house where I live. Each protest's end point is much easier to assign, though the protestation often dissipates the obsessive need for assigning. But, in reference to the endpoint of the early September protest, I can say that it came at 6:45 pm, since it is in the late light of the day and across long shadows cast by the sun in the West that my worries subside. Then, with a sense of elation that I don't find comical, I can hit my stride. The foot is an astonishing instrument, absorbing shocks, bending and flexing as it adjusts to the terrain and carries its burden on. In much current avant-garde poetry, theory and practice have become largely implicated in each other's creative and critical projects, such that one can often discern (though perhaps not separately locate) the critical/analytic features of a poem or the poetic features of a work of critical theorizing. The result is not necessarily a new genre, and, if and when it is, that is not what is significant about it. What is important is the emergence of a new precise but expansive method ——— a new, socio-aesthetic approach to the uses and understandings of language. This is an urban development; writing has become consciously, even perhaps conscientiously, social.

> I looked into my vagina
> And what did I see?
> Eggs in a nest
> In a family tree.

Whatever the shock value of avant-garde art and regardless of whatever deracinating pressures it exerts on society, even while it is more descriptive than prophetic, there is nonetheless a real future in it. Real things will show up ——— people and garden snails and neologisms, mortality and sparrows and an occasional bulldog or poodle, and disappointment verging on outrage. Desire makes a deal with dust and it affects us readily and weirdly when we get really ——— indeed, in reality ——— close to the surface of a thing and squint ourselves into an orgy of contemplation until we feel we are engaging in thrilling inter-species communications. Askari Nate Martin is now thinking he should be feeling ethically unburdened or actively interested or able to dance with abandon, he is feeling unprofited. Significant aesthetic works take people out of their comfort zone but so do urban battlefields, sacrifice zones, crime scenes. Almost any-one can gain access to a poem, but only members of a professional elite are admitted to the scene of a murder or plane crash, and only members of a financial elite can gamble with the fortunes of a society. Odyn, dos, trois, four, fumf, hat, septus, ocht, ni, sampu! Here we come, ready or not. You laugh? Bridges abound or the bridges are out. I'm not convinced that it's the writer's responsibility to build the boat and craft the oars that can carry her readers from imaginative possibility to reality and back again. Or is it reality we begin with. It's not a matter of access only but also of comprehensibility ———— knowledge, in effect, and cognizance of something's mattering. It's never a perfectly round trip, either way. At what point does a reader accept an invitation to embark? All literature, not just avant-garde literature, needs readers. Writers can make their works accessible, but that doesn't mean that readers should come. Mikhail Epstein has proposed that literary prizes should be awarded to readers, not writers. Annual prizes for the year's best reader of poetry, the best reader of philosophical texts, of travel memoirs, of history, anthropology, fiction, and so forth would be awarded at an annual ceremony. And, in due course, if there's sufficient prize money, the fiction category could be subdivided into genres, allowing for an annual award for the given year's best reader of detective novels, romances, Westerns, spy novels, as well as literary fiction and porn. How does a reader understand the contexts and pressures, or the hopes, or frustrations, or griefs, or joys, or angers that the writer feels, passionately or tacitly or manipulatively or playfully or wishfully, as he or she wrote the work? Actually, the question to ask before this one is: how does the writer know what he or she is putting into the work? We hardly know what we are putting into life. And yet we put things in, and are unwilling, and per-haps unable, not to do so. As Spinoza notes, "Not even men well versed in affairs can keep silent [...]. It is the common failing of men to confide what they think to others, even when secrecy is needed." One could argue, perhaps, that one possible intention of avant-garde poetry is to obliterate secrecy, so that nothing in it is the outcome of a compulsion to tell. I weed a tiny backyard garden, sweep a kitchen, answer e-mail, admire my cat, fail to come up with a title for an essay, buy some groceries, and in the late afternoon am suddenly touched by the poignancy of the breeze's shifting light through the leaves of trees at the edge of a playground. Everyday life (adhesive repetition) is both definite and indefinite, accessible and inaccessible. The same could be said of the persons we love. There is no avant-garde of love. I can only hope that what I don't say is best said by not being said. O sun on the avant-garde. "I thought that if I could put it all down, that would be one way. And next the thought came to me that to leave all out would be another, and truer, way." Perhaps encyclopedic ambitions are best fulfilled unsystematically. Consciousness should leap to resumptions, rather than conclusions. Continuities aren't smooth. But the avant-garde rushes forward self-sacrificially, precisely to create the negative space in which an unforeseen future might find a place. And this takes time. Even, sometimes, the slow time that consciousness registers when one is falling from a great height or proceeding toward a collision with a truck or tree, every detail of each remaining millisecond getting noted and set in place for memory. Why should the understanding of a work of art be a sudden thing, like a seizure: "I get it!" No doubt it helps to approach a work of art with information, but what's far more important is curiosity, liveliness, patience, and trust. Alfred North Whitehead is said to have "trusted brutal transitions and unexpected coexistences." If a mathematician can do so, why can't a reader of poetry? Along comes a pigeon, along come Alice Milligan Webster and Constance Otto Donegan, along comes a helicopter and in comes the fog. It's 4:30 pm. Sometimes it suffices to say "along comes X or Y," but that a reader is feeling the fullness of the amazing fact that X or Y is coming along is hard to assess. "The nursery governor flew back into the well / With the little figure without hands in the brown-tree clothes." So ends Thomas MacGreevy's "Homage to Hieronymus Bosch." Bosch's images are said to be "grotesque." When he painted a pheasant, it might have been pressing a penis to its feathered breast. When he painted a peasant, it might have been a raucous warty woman on ice skates named Corinda or a man named Glaucous John as round as a planet and exerting equal gravity. Life is serious, and art should be too. Sadly, it can't be sufficiently serious, nor abundant enough, to counteract injustice, cruelty, or the numerous forms of war. Wars are heavily capitalized, lavishly underwritten, and patently merchandized. The citizenry has to be sold on them, and then the citizens can be sold news of them. Wars become rapidly accessible. So sadly the women stare at the hills, the malls, their shoes, their children's shoes, the rivers. I dream of boards that are made of words instead of wood ——— "sayings": colorful slats composed of graffiti, white, pink, aquamarine (the colors with which kitsch seashell objets are decorated). The walls of the subsequent shack, built of these words/boards, are fissured with cracks; the shack is cold and public. I come to this profound conclusion about the nature of language: everything by virtue of it is permeable. Then I dream of a beach; in the dream the word for it is plague, then plage, then page. But I no longer have dreams like that. Dreams are false secrets. That dream is locally trapped in the running after names. Or that dream is vocally lapped by competing names. Kiss could cap, standing doubt history: I can feel it! To advocate for an art that upsets expectations so as to keep (or render) life lively ——— isn't that tantamount to putting bourgeois individuality and bourgeois modes of happiness at the center of the aesthetic agenda and implying that the exercise, on the one hand, and appreciation, on the other, of individual genius are among the "rights of man"? As Marx says, after reviewing the North American Declaration of Independence, Declaration of the Rights of Man, and Constitution, "Not one of the so-called rights of man goes beyond egoistic man [...], namely an individual withdrawn into himself, his private interest and his private desires and separated from the community. [...] Citizenship, the political community, is reduced by the political emancipators to a mere means for the conservation of these so-called rights of man and [...] the citizen is therefore proclaimed the servant of egoistic man; [...] the sphere in which man behaves as a communal being is degraded to a level below the sphere in which he behaves as a partial being, and finally [...] it is man as <u>bourgeois</u> [...] and not man as citizen who is taken as the <u>real</u> and <u>authentic</u> man." Difficult art works, just as much as those that are reassuring, may be complicit in advancing the egoism of the reluctant citizen, but he or she isn't necessarily in charge. What are you doing? Are you crazy? Are you playing some stupid game? Go ahead, keep digging your stupid holes, I'm out of here! Injustice amuses itself in many ways. So it is that a homeless woman, dining on scraps from a restaurant's garbage, vomits the nutrition away. Passersby indulge their "prurient curiosity," the inane and banal behavior ——— the observant passivity ——— typical of spectators at a fire or the scene of a car crash. They watch in bad faith, carrying out an invasion of privacy, so as to exact vicarious experience from others' lives and indulge in emotions they haven't earned. Bad lyric poets do the same. And even the ordinary voyeur intervenes in a given temporal flow. The Futurists wanted to speed everything up ——— to outrace boredom, predictability, pattern, history ——— and the Minimalists wanted to strip away perception of speed altogether. A. J. Wiertz, a 19th-century Belgian painter, writes in 1870, "The human spirit begins to accustom itself to the power of matter." Out of this accustomization to matter's power, tantamount to fascination or even obsession with it, art for art's sake emerges. What current power will shape the art of the near future, or is shaping it now? Perhaps it is something like the power of fear. A medium-range ballistics missile is sent eastward in the late afternoon and destroys a shopping complex. The members of the response team, wearing night-vision goggles, dig through the debris in a dreamy state. All hours on the battlefront are equal: 60 minutes of war. Or maybe it <u>is</u> just a game. A parent who wants to watch a movie to see whether it is suitable for a child can readily do so, but video games are layered, and it is impossible to gain immediate access to their full contents; you have to play through the layers, kill some cyphers, blow up some blocks, before you can kill a cop, then burn a woman. "No parent," some pundit in a radio interview says, "can just play the game for an hour or two and know what the game has to offer, what experiences are to come." The windows are open, the shadows jumping away from the sunlight are producing chaotic patterns on the sidewalk and street, moving bands and bulges, sliding back and forth over the dull cement, the rough asphalt, the dirt and weeds edging the curb, the hood of a car. A pedestrian flings her shadow slightly ahead of herself and onto the wall of a building as she goes by. Intuition, which is so closely bound to desire, knows immediately that the shadows are produced by sunlight and each thing that impedes its rays; analysis articulates that knowledge, recognizes the pleasure provoked by it, knows that desire is flowing, and, in the descriptions that follow, is likely to add embellishments. "There is no desire more natural than the desire for knowledge," writes Montaigne at the beginning of the essay "Of experience." "We try all the ways that can lead us to it. When reason fails us, we use experience." A reader's encounter with a difficult (impenetrable or impervious) text can produce a sense of frustration or even of outrage, a sense that he or she is being barred from knowledge and from the meaning that flows from it. Unwilling to surrender to alienation, the reader, when experience fails, tries reason.

19

A painting sets out to "attract the beholder, then to arrest and finally enthrall the beholder." It must "call to someone, bring him to a halt in front of itself and hold him there as if spellbound and unable to move." So, at least, says Michael Fried in Absorption and Theatricality. He is making a polemical point and I have no desire to take him to task for it. And, indeed, I've been, so to speak, hailed by paintings in just this way. By the paintings, not by the painter. But attributing authority to a painting, or imagining that to endow the painting with authority was among its painter's intentions, assumes that works of art can take on an independent existence, severed from their making (whether by the artist or the audience) ———— severed from poeisis. If this were the case, paintings would be frozen into façades, mortally allegorical. It is by virtue of the active force of their manner that the paintings of Pierre Bonnard, and particularly the late interiors and still lifes, move us to impossible perception, uncertain consideration, "permanently delaying ———— even foiling ———— a unifying synthesis by keeping things fluid, by keeping contradictions actively unresolved, choices indefinitely postponed." I should explain what I meant a month or two ago when I referred to the (ungodlike) phenomenological face of Rosario Basho Clark's painting. The painting mobilizes the surface of Rosario Basho Clark's ubiquitous ambient concerns. Characters in a scenario come into play through that mobility ———— present, available, though not always objectively perceptible ———— though the surface never entirely recedes. "That's the shit, Rosario," says Commando. Near the bottom third of the painting on the left, on bare canvas above a smear of dark blue disappearing into an amorphous patch of delicate red, safe from the incursions of heavy paint that initially seems to dominate the canvas, is a meticulously drawn small scene in which three boys are gathered beside a bicycle, two of them observing, one of whom is awkwardly holding what looks like a wrench, while the third is apparently attending to the gears or the chain. Meanwhile, just to the right of the center of the painting, where swathes of dark red, ochre, blue, and brown paint have been laid onto the canvas is another scene, this one a landscape of high-rises on a waterfront, even the textures of the buildings' walls are minutely etched, as is the rigging on a crane looming over the dock, and the containers on the deck of a cargo ship. And near the top of the painting, in a patch not quite free of paint, is a third but much rougher drawing, this one a portrait, or partial portrait, since the left side of the face has been swept into a passage of dark red. But not everything that happens in one's life gets into one's conscious account of it. Works of art are compendia of knowledge, with never-sufficient indicative space in them to absorb reality. In the streaks and whorls of paint there are many possible face forms —— avian, mammalian, floral —— though they are all so miniscule and muddled and multiple that I should doubt whether they are in the painting (and, so to speak, objectively real) or, instead, exist solely in the visual reading I'm imposing on it, as one imposes dinosaurs, rabbits, ogres, and so forth on clouds, thick foliage, or in water stains on a wall, or heroines in a cluster, visible only peripherally, from Earth of stars. I remember something Charlie Altieri said. It was in a conversation, then he wrote it down: "When we emote, we enter another world." Wearing a mask of aspiration, or of inattention, or of earnestness, or accomplishment, or invisibility, or need, or of any other of the myriad aspects one turns to the world, a figure leaps into view, whether in aggression or glee I can't tell, and I throw my hands in front of my face. Our awareness of reality is stimulated by movements within it (blowing leaves, children at play, dog chasing a squirrel, shift of fabric at wrist, approaching bus), and, more importantly, by what Alfred North Whitehead calls the "quality of passage." The problems of empathy, sympathy, affinity remain unresolved. Francesca Malaya Martin is sprinkling sugar over a bowl of strawberries. The masterpieces of Vermeer are sentimental because in them Vermeer hasn't included inattention. The masterpieces of Rembrandt, in which moment and manner of execution are the very matter of the paintings, emerging from things that are discerned but remain not quite discernible, are about sensation rather than sentiment. Rembrandt paints not the state of things but their conditions. Change is prominent among them, but we can only perceive it indirectly and comparatively, on uncertain grounds, while it is happening also to us. Likeness is reduced to the smallest possible importance, and effectiveness ——— effectfulness ——— is dependent on difference. Difference triumphs over identity. Pushpin, island, lead balloon, alphabet, cellos pianissimo, then ribaldry and plurals; manner becomes event. "Though the sun always shines literally in the sense that it emits rays of light, it is usually not considered beautiful in itself. The beauty of sunshine seems, rather, to depend on indirection: the shimmer of silver linings on clouds, the shine of dawn light on a landscape, the way a sun's ray passes through the clouds, the reflection of a winter sun on a lake." Through the open window a sequence of sounds is audible from the street, as of someone shaking coins in a heavy metal box, then of something like the resonant knocking of cut logs as they are tossed onto a woodpile, then of horses trotting through a shallow creek over gravel, but none of these are the likely sources of the passing sounds, which in any case are now fading away. What we perceive is passage, the events of things, moving, at the moment, through a relative silence harboring the sometimes complacent, sometimes anxious or insistent, sometimes bilious or mournful cooing of pigeons nesting under the eaves of the building next-door. But it isn't always pertinent to reconcile manner with matter. Doing so doesn't necessarily give us an advantage ——— we being members of a species that has a strong proclivity for setting up advantages and then seizing them. We call that "creativity" or "innovation" and learn something of the matter and manner of some things in the world, things inhabiting the plot of the world. What are we missing? At some point, after a period of naked life, a heroine in particular feels suddenly in need of what she calls "carapace" ——— her own, and probably yours and mine, too, but she carefully avoids calling attention to that, the blank of the who in the now what. Toward the end of <u>Les Misérables</u>, Victor Hugo describes a shift in the attitudes of the disenfranchised, oppressed, impoverished, imprisoned, from mournfulness and abjection to rage and "a diabolic enigmatic gaiety": "All the songs... were humble and sad to the point of tears. The underworld calls itself the poor pègre, and it is always the hare in hiding, the mouse escaping, the bird flying off. It scarcely complains, it merely sighs.... The miserable being, whenever he has time to reflect, imagines himself insignificant before the law and wretched before society; he prostrates himself, he begs, he turns toward pity; we feel that he sees himself in the wrong. Toward the middle of the last century, there was a change. The prison songs, the robbers' ritornels, took on an insolent and jovial expression. The plaintive maluré was supplanted by the larifla." However angry, inventive, imaginative, uproarious, or rambunctious the anti-capitalist protestors may be, the corporate interests ignore them, much in the way that a conquering army ignores the dogs barking at its heels, their clamor producing nothing more than proof that the conquerors are going by, hauling away their spoils. Maggie Fornetti, Jean Day, Tanya Smith, Dewanda Horn, Greg Levine, Ricardo Gomez and I bark with the others. Capitalism has no central headquarters. The protestors are disappointingly few, but it's early in the semester, momentum has yet to build. A small group of protestors is gathering in front of the public buildings in the "revitalized city center." Harsh sunlight is reflected off its new, monolithic, pale façades, offering nothing but the blind, undreamy, indifferent gaze said properly to belong to a god. "Nobody don't like everybody," says Flip. "When I get into shit it's my shit, know what I'm saying?" Askari Nate Martin picks up his cell phone, it's almost 1 pm, a text message from Maggie Fornetti says she's "5 blx away." "That's right," says Carlotta. Outside the Oakland MAP storefront on 17th Street, Askari Nate Martin nods at Constantine Otto Donegan. They can hear the sounds of chanting protestors a few blocks away. Constantine Otto Donegan has sprained the middle finger of his right hand; he winces as he puts on his jacket and laughs as if at the petty foibles of life.

20

Much has been said against description, as against representation, ascription, or the production of spectacles. I'm not here to defend description, nor to defend myself against it (though we would all do well to be wary of it, and of the apparatuses of surveillance through which, as if it were news, or a beast of prey from a bush, description breaks). Even when their intentions are benevolent, even when they explore or caress, descriptions are never entirely innocent. There is always something lustful lurking in them ——— however dreamily. One has to guard against one's will to description, even as one situates or names or hails the things one sees. Charlie Altieri speaks of "the muted but persistent pain occurring when the imagination can do nothing with the world but describe it." This pain is more a problem for poets than for writers of narrative fiction, but certainly Proust suffered from it, and George Eliot, Melville, and Virginia Woolf. Charles Dickens's descriptions are so much a part of the stories in which they occur that they can scarcely be extrapolated from them. They are almost always offered from the perspective of a character ———or a projection of Dickens's knowledge of the character, a knowledge that is informed by judgments he has already passed. W.J.T. Mitchell speaks of "'lost objects' or 'part objects' that we must fetishistically repossess to make ourselves whole," elegantly describing commodity-desire: <u>my day/life/world won't be complete until I have X!</u> But might this not also pertain to our relationship to certain features of a cherished landscape or to certain works of art, which we possess spiritually, or totemically, incorporating them into our (assumed) identity? <u>I love the San Francisco fog!</u> <u>I love Bonnard!</u> Such statements declare one's secret, or a component of the secret that sits at the core of one's singularity. Here particularity is at one with solemnity, individuality with mourning. But then the world appears, dispersing coherence. Coleridge's account in "This Lime-Tree Bower My Prison" of a walk that some friends are taking without him "To that still roaring dell, of which I told" imagines a prospect, laid out by memory, and occasioned (literally) by pain, though not of the sort that Charlie Altieri is referring to (Coleridge's wife, "dear Sara," had spilled a skillet of boiling milk on his foot). In the poem's last line, Coleridge states that "No sound is dissonant which tells of Life," but the tone throughout is melancholic, almost elegiac. Perhaps this is inevitable. Descriptions tend to be commemorative, in effect if not in intention, as if tacit knowledge of the things of the world were disappearing. In the context of their depiction, they are proffered for sharing one last time. But even as they come into view, so to speak, we sense the world as one whose things are silently separating from each other. "Heat is the consequence of light (cats sleep under parked cars), the old women look small & bundled, wrapped in overcoats on their way to mass (I hear a rooster crow in the city)." Thus begins the second part of Ron Silliman's four-part poem "Skies." What we have here is as much compilation as description. In his brief note on the work, Silliman explains his method starkly: "Every day for one year I looked at the sky & noted what I saw." What time of year is it? A few sentences (days) later "schoolkids & clericals bunch at the bus stop," so summer is over. It's late September, a few weeks past Labor Day, or early October, which is when the San Francisco Bay Area experiences its own "summer" season, buffeted by the hot Diablo wind. And it is over seasons, not time, that the skies of Silliman's title hover, providing cover for the shapes that come to his attention. Space has a formative character when it accumulates within and around a description. Its ambiguity, even ambivalence, becomes an active force in generating comprehension of what's being described, on the part of both reader/auditor and describer. On the one hand, the space in or of the description has to contain at least some familiar elements ——— we have to be able to place what's being described, to frame it. And so the space of a description has to maintain stability. And yet the space in or of a description is also infinitely unstable. That's what descriptions do ——— they summon circumstances into the transience of our awareness of them, reminding us of the imaginariness, provisionality, improvisatory nature of our constructions ——— all of them: our "things." And of our alarming reluctance to let them fall apart, to let them go. Descriptions make circumstantiality available to consciousness and circumstances a source of memory. Most of the materials that drift into an autobiography are created long after the fact, but some are created in advance of what we desire or fear. Without removing his earbuds, so he might just be talking to himself, Russell Wright says, "Facts are like habits, and habits are just limitations." But habits, though definitive, can be self-determining, rather than self-limiting, and more expressive than we realize. Admittedly, it is not out of emotion (and especially not out of desire) but out of habit that one dresses in the morning, eats, pisses, grimaces, grins, drinks a cup of strong coffee. One's customary way of doing things doesn't generally accomplish much. "It's hard to know if any reality can stick to it," says Russell Wright, scanning the view for a moment; "reality only brushes over the surface of things." But, at least in part, it's in following our familiar routines, what have come to be our particular habitual ways of moving through each day, that we are ourselves. As animal and chemical and electric beings, we exercise what Manuel De Landa calls "a flexible behavioral repertoire" and "enter into complex combinations with heterogeneous elements." But we do this naturally, so to speak; these are things we just do. Grapefruits on display at the supermarket belong to the reality of always already described things. I select a good one all but unconsciously, its rosy-yellow bumpy skin is firm and tight. There are things I know without bothering to know I know them, elements in a shadow world. But presumably those shadows are a sign of life. Freud's attention to dream life ———— or to the linguistic and pictorial objects that his dreamer-patients recount ———— emerges precisely at the time that consumer culture is emerging, with its proliferation of commodities. This is not merely coincidental. The psychic life of the bourgeoisie, including that of Freud and his patients, was becoming home to things with a life of their own ———— comforting or mysterious, compelling or horrific. They were seizing knowledge to themselves.

But maybe Things should be loved.
Perhaps Things have different souls from ours.
(Mayakovsky)

Low hills slowly rise to the east of College Avenue. Idly I caress
a tiny patch of dry skin on the wrinkled back of my left hand
with my right forefinger, then notice dirt under its nail and fold
the forefinger down, out of view. The parataxis of value (no
one thing more important than another) doesn't level the emo-
tional landscape, and doesn't decrease one's embarrassment at
odd moments of self-encounter. The chain of associations is a
daisy chain. Wherever the set of a doorknob or the butter on
a slice of toast expresses an attitude, the work that went into
it shows. The same is true of the sneer of a schoolgirl, whose
work on herself has met an impediment. Tamarind Magee has
lost her story, she's got no traction, all she can do is slide into
place on an empty bench. The seat doesn't provide her with any
real point of view, but, she says, "I'm done with being driven."
We are ——— at least for the moment ——— who knows what
we will turn into? who knows what we were last? ——— fated
to be human. The rest of reality is not independent of us, but
not dependent on us, either. It is not entirely extra-human, and
it is neither ahistorical nor otherwise transcendent. It is a given;
the ivory-white walls of the room in which I'm sitting to record
this (or to imagine it ——— if that's any different) are not an
illusion. And they aren't irrelevant. Nor were the tiny roses on
the green floral wallpaper of my childhood bedroom and the
sound of the vacuum cleaner as my mother ran it over the hall-
way floor, which was benign in the daylight, though at night
in the dark, as the house shifted, it provided the surface for
creaks, groans, and the prowling of a population of indistinct
enemies, persecutors. Tamarind Magee says "prosecutors." She
is encountering a paradox that she is too young to experience
as anything other than hers alone. Continuity is discontinuous.
Tamarind Magee is in a discontinuous relation with herself. But
individuality is not undone when it loses or gains characteristics,
context, experiences. Individuality is substantively indiscrete,
and subjectivity is significantly promiscuous. Tamarind Magee
has energy; she turns and looks at me. Description can't pretend

to stand in for meaning nor even to establish or verify presence. The soundtrack in the lobby of the small mall at the edge of the plaza pumps out, at low volume, the sounds of an android singing "Mexican monkey" (really? can that be what the words are?) backed up by a percussion machine. Uh, uh-uh O. I try to set my fingers to an F chord on the guitar and my left wrist quivers. On College Avenue, a group of people, I among them, pass each other, and I, in my usual haste —— or age-defiant vigor? —— am impatiently passing everyone, hurrying, parallel to the sea, from which yellow balls are being lobbed toward us. Phloup. Buong. I am playing catch with the sea. From maximum of monstrous intensity to sniffle of reach reality and back again to ineffable egress and back to withdrawn denial from interlocking of cups and stones and back to blue facet of abandon from modest lantern on the ground and immodest canvas scale. After awhile I notice that everyone who steps back to catch a sun steps into the way of passing cars and disappears. We are being killed off. Day is done, yes, and day has won.

21

Every work of art attests to lived experience and reminds us that another human has been here. Echoes aren't inherently empty. The emotional encounter —— the felt awareness of something other that is essentially a memory, but one emitted, as it were, by another —— is crucial for our consciousness of history and a key to the good life. But it is in this way, too, that Death makes its appearance in a work of art. I'll get to the quandary of the good life later. Inadequately, but that may be for the best. In Goya's great painting The Third of May 1808, we see before us a moment just before an execution. Already three lifeless bodies are lying in pools of blood on the ground, and now, kneeling beside them but with his hands held high (some critics say "like Christ," but I don't think so —— why is "like Christ" an enhancement of who he is?), is the next victim —— a powerful man, with a mustache and thick curly hair, wearing a startlingly white blouse and trousers as yellow as sunlight. The sky is black; this is happening at night, or in Hell. With a look as much of sorrow as of fear or anger, the powerful man glares at the men, factotums of the firing squad. There are at least five of them, left foot forward and right foot back, faces hidden (they are wearing shakos and are turned slightly away from us), the long barrels of their rifles raised and thrust forward, jabbing inhumanity, or dishumanity, into the middle of the painting. On the ground, at the center of the scene, and casting luminous light on the man who is about to be shot, is a large square lantern —— it must be at least two feet tall and equally wide. It's a yellow lantern, the color of the condemned man's pants. Its light casts forth the white of the condemned man's shirt. Picasso is reported to have said, "The lantern is Death. Why? We don't know." Reconciling the good life (whatever we might mean by that) with mortality is one of humanity's many failed undertakings. Slaughter, assassination, war, injustice —— or sheer immiseration —— are the most prevalent forms that overtake this reconciliation. I am writing this at home, three doors down from the corner of College Avenue and Russell Street. In my home state currently (August 2013), there are 727 individuals on death row, awaiting execution. In Florida, which has the next largest population of condemned men and women, there are 413. Life shudders at the edges of imagination, its aperture, perhaps its exit. The sun is taking up another of its innumerable positions. A few healthy clouds seem immobile below it, but in fact they are simply being pulled along as the earth rolls slowly clockwise. If it went any faster I would never get this paragraph finished. Some of the persons on death row must regard themselves as all but dead; they can't easily regard themselves as living life. Their situation is one of acute tension, but it's devoid of enlivening intensity. Facing execution, some acquiesce, some resist, some feel contrition and apologize, some deny wrongdoing. All have a gray, limited space to stare into. Most have a lawyer. Some of those lawyers long to be acknowledged as the spiritual source of a prisoner's repentance ———— which the lawyers imagine as the threshold of freedom (of which immortality is the ultimate condition); they are not lacking in imagination, but the prisoner is at their mercy. By offering repentance while rejecting his or her lawyer, the death row prisoner exercises what in many cases is the only power he or she has left. To shift context requires context-consciousness, to recuperate experience from the condition of postness in its abject manifestation as, paradoxically, pastlessness. Living presences ———— bodies (human, rock, pine, pigeon, desk, delphinium) ———— together broaden the shadow in which life is possible. What's needed, then, is an unbordering. Something including but beyond the evaluative or juridical, and something more than aesthetic, certainly, and more than nocturnal (obscure and dreamy), and something beyond synthesis, and perhaps slightly paranormal ———— but if that, then why not also paranoid? Well, because paranoia evaporates, or becomes unthinkable, in the processes of outspreading, when it's impossible to affix motives and orient them to oneself, narcissistically, as it were. Paranoid subjectivity is as abyssal as fear, swallowing everything up. I experienced something that seems to me to have demonstrated a reversal of narcissism. It was in a recent dream ———— and just before dawn of a Monday morning. I'd fallen asleep to the looping through my thoughts of the phrase "I aspired to something blasphemous" ——— I, who am not even capable of brutal honesty! I can't forgive humanity its physical monstrosity, but mostly because I can't bring myself to openly acknowledge it. A stocky black dog comes around the corner in front of LULULEMON ATHLETICA, trotting beside a man who says its name is Snake, "because it is blatantly phallic." The woman with him contradicts him blandly: "her name is Buttercup." The dog shrinks, condenses, becoming a frog. It leaps at me, scattering water, and becomes an armadillo. In this form, it evokes the word peccadillo. Then it explodes, in a burst of multi-colored floral fireworks ——— a pyrotechnic peony. Tolstoy, on May 12, 1856, after years of using his diary principally to castigate himself and draft rules for self-improvement, writes: "the best way to true happiness in life is to have no rules, but to throw out from yourself in all directions like a spider a prehensile web of love and catch in it everything that comes along ——— an old lady, a child, a woman, or a policeman." In this sudden effusion he deploys a metaphor that is both predatory and radiant to express a burst of charitable feeling. His purpose is not predation, however, but embrace. To connect is to accept, and to remember, but with centrifugal force. Tolstoy's moment of love, insofar as it casts all of itself outward, resembles a moment of dying. It is the opposite of encyclopedic; it's discyclopedic. It's a moment in which time ——— even temporality itself ——— loses its coherence. We could liken it to the sound of a piano chord, its sun-blasted sphericity and experimental off-rhyming, whose effects pulse and oscillate as if to remind us that the espousal of art for art's sake doesn't tell us what art's sake is. Aestheticism at this level brings with it a kind of madness, dazzling as an ornament. It adds something allegorical to what it produces. And that allegory's value lies in its vitality, not in its beauty; it plays out socially, introducing new comparisons and thus new conditions, new criteria, new ways of seeing one thing as another. And, as T.J. Clark reminds us, "[W]ildness and otherness are always just there in the world [...] ——— part of our ordinary nonidentity, part of everyday life." There's no real need for us to supplement our perceptions, they receive our additions in an instant. Living things can arrange themselves into pictures as much as pictures can depict living things. Or, to put it another way, living things may serve as signs, and ——— in protest actions, for example ——— as signs for pictures, arrayed in an indexical spin.

> Alphabet, use of apple in
> Barrel, rotten apple in
> Code, alpha for apple in
> Dapple, apple rhymes with
> Eden, apple not really the fruit in
> Fall, apple falsely figures in man's
> Gloss, apple red lip
> Horse, apple a treat for a
> Index, apples an early fruit in
> Jelly, mint apple
> Kitsch, apple pie as American
> Lore, apple in folk
> Meter, apple in trochaic
> Nostril, apple-like tip of the
> Oranges, apples and
> Pie, apple
> Quality, Red Delicious apples of uneven
> Ready, apples in autumn are
> Seed, Johnny Apple
> Tomato, love apple another name for
> Unctuousness, apples misused to express
> Vigor, apples said to increase
> Witch, apple used to poison Snow White by
> Xanadu, incense of apples not unlikely in
> Ylang-ylang, fragrant custard-apple tree called the
> Zarathustra, eagle brings a sweet-scented rosy
>   apple to

A cold wind pushes against the northward progress of the occasional pedestrian, a plastic wrapper slips past a parking meter and disappears under a red car. In Minima Moralia, Adorno remarks, "To happiness the same applies as to truth: one does not have it, but is in it." But what if the truth one is in ——— the truth of one's situation or of one's entire epoch ——— is an untruth: a lie, a fabrication, a myth, or a lack of truth altogether; not just a figment of false consciousness but the very condition that produces it? Certainly such a truth-of-one's-time would be an unhappiness. Adorno's aphorism, then, with a slight adjustment (and added poignancy) would assert that to unhappiness the same applies as to untruth: one does not have it, but is in it. It's not the wind but the sun that expands the neighborhood through which vehicles, pedestrians, pets, children, residents, bugs, birds, visitors, bacteria, move in their efforts at perfection. The dark of night expands the neighborhood, too. "It was dark, the sidewalk was going fast, then it turned into a bunch of kids, and everything exploded," says Connie Donegan, and Nate looks at Connie's profile. "That's what the witness says," Connie continues. "Her words. Bunny Victoria Zander, age 17, white. She was bicycling home from a party." In the background, like markings on the face of a boulder but more fleetingly interpretable, are the sounds of a speeding motorcycle, a jackhammer, a crow, a pedestrian's laughter, a day laborer tugging open a bag of tortilla chips. At times the human world can barely hold together, but small patterns of interrelated events circulate through it. E orders another beer, L pats his arm, D goes to pee. As Michael Fried notes, "[I]n the mode of everydayness not only is the whole not greater than the sum of the parts, it is also not exactly what we tend to think of as a whole (or indeed as a sum [...])." Art historians generally seem to be better at seeing the quiddities of everyday life than literary critics, who read into depictions of it coherences that are essentially irrelevant to the everyday. Apertures expand, sprawl over the edges of a frame. Thinking generates turmoil, something entirely different from entropy, it doesn't settle and it doesn't resolve, unless briefly, so the thinker can take a breather. Meanwhile, in the thinking, tension builds. An excess of spirit suffuses the body, it contorts the face, which is seen to convulse, either in laughter or in grief. Some human feels it in the stomach ——— a tightening, reflux, pain in the solar plexus. Some cat wakes suddenly. The cat launches its mouth at its haunch, licking, nibbling (affectionately, it seems). A horse shies, bucks, veers, and drops its head to graze. Deer, reclining in a meadow, leap to their feet and flee. How do I release tension? Not very well. A glass of wine. Currently, despite my sympathy for Tolstoy's charitable impulse, I could not readily include a policeman in any "prehensile web of love" I might cast. Though we feel liberated at the conventional end of a fairy tale ("and they lived happily ever after"), we are aware of anxiety lurking along the fraying edges of "ever after," where existence continues beyond the scope of what's told, and perhaps beyond the scope of what can be told. Goethe's last words were, so they say, "More light." I could imagine a variant of these: "More sleep." But those are mere words, and a translation, at that, and not even last words, as more words have followed since, including those that proclaim them "last." Mercilessly.

22

In The Practice of Everyday Life, Michel de Certeau describes walking in the city as an experience of utter rootlessness. "The moving about that the city multiplies and concentrates makes the city itself an immense social experience of lacking a place." But surely what de Certeau is describing must depend on where one is in the city. What, for example, if one were in one's own neighborhood? Wouldn't one have a sense of belonging there (perhaps with a concomitant sense of who doesn't belong ——— a levying of prejudicial judgments). Or perhaps we don't walk in cities at all, we ramble ——— or stumble ——— in the global economy, cheeks brushed by the petro-breeze, eyes on apps. The poet-scholar writes a poem, or it might be an essay; she quotes contemporary intellectual authorities, alludes to current influential ideas. The professional professor scoffs: "You come well-defended, Poet; you have brought artillery." She is wrong. As a knife in language, there sticks the tongue. An event occurs ——— it's an achievement of the temporal flow we call space. It isn't only then and there, or now and here; it is happening. Everyday life (attributed repetition) is lived by habit, of course, and yet it is also a realm of decisions, choices, and thus, in some sense, it's an ethical sphere: the realm of living with one's choices, along with the choices made by others. Everyday life (switched repetition) has multiple centers of gravity, various data draw our attention, and we are individually diverted. But in querying everyday life from an anarcho-socialist perspective, there are two questions to ask: what makes people happy, and what makes people unhappy? Sean Bonney writes (in Happiness):

> [...]
> it is thin, our cynicism, the latest distinct word
> sometimes, when a specific distortion in the vowels is
>   achieved   ·
> we can hear heaven. It is a kind of wall

all of our clear, musical nouns
the morality of our achievements, singing on the
    scaffold
& the riot squad have denied everything
our laws and our tastes, this is harmony
[...]

In a bookstore, as at a supermarket, driving in traffic, walking on city streets, one is constantly (though mostly unconsciously) making quick decisions about the relevance to oneself of all that's happening. It rained during the night. At last. The sky is still cloudy, gray, though not, at the moment, "threatening." Guardian pumpkins glow at doorways, grinning, grimacing, scowling, voracious. The windows are open, and the scent of damp pavement, humid soil, foliage, building façades wafts in, the breeze brushing my face just as my eyes and read-ing mind come to the beginning of a sentence in Isabelle Stengers's Thinking with Whitehead, "The conveyance of some sense-objects by others might one day…," and I raise my head, the sentence slants away, scent in the air of the air, the sur-feit of something before finishing. Memory provokes a ready pathos, present in the complex sensations that accrue around the fact of one's having lived. The fact moves, like the float-ers in my eyes, as hard to track as the stars in the Pleiades, or like a coincidence, with its moving parts. The sounds and smells and touchings in the air socialize. It's that that adds to the emotional thrill of memory. That thrill isn't always a happy one. Memory can pinch at one's world. Charlie Altieri rubs his elbow. I return to the text.

[...]
every possible combination of peoples and phantoms
our sobriety and victims, this is our alphabet
sometimes, we get sick of our pious barbarism
we leap screeching into hell
our immense, unquestionable affluence

Bonney's poem as published might be an unrhymed, unmetered sonnet; it fulfills what appears to be the minimal requirement of having fourteen lines. It is one of a number of Bonney's poems in the book said to be "after Rimbaud," and there's something of Rimbaud's precocity, distress, and ambivalence in it ——— "the feeling," as Angus Fletcher notes, that "one experiences in situations of acute social tension," whose impact/structure is allegorical: "allegory always demonstrates a degree of inner conflict, which we call 'ambivalence.'" I ask Charlie Altieri, "May I introduce you as a character in my poem/essay/story?" He says, "Your energy is amazing ——— or maybe appalling." Or that's what he might say; the act of description, which, if it is honestly carried out, is as much a perceptual process as anything else, and comes, ultimately, to an arbitrary end. But in its course, in saying what things are, or what things are said, the process may sometimes discover also why things are, and why they are said. On the other hand, it can reflect rank superstition. "One of the strongest proofs of the irrationality of human beings is that they look for reason where it is not to be found. They look for intention in chance, and, since they know well that this intention is not theirs, they presume that it is another's." Every description, no matter how assiduously carried out, flirts with secrecy, which, like the red that's said of the robin's breast, deepens the surface of the description's main clause, its central proposition. Relative clauses, on the other hand, have a captioning effect: the real estate boom that brought logs pounding into the city; Alexander Pope, whose stature was "that of a 12-year-old boy"; the neighbor, who is throwing walnuts at passing cars; a seafaring bobcat, which comes out of the waves; Alexander Pope, whose name became attached to a figure fleeting through my dream one night riding a bird, because, perhaps, Maynard Mack, in his biography of Pope, commenting on Pope's sex life, says, "The wren goes to 't with as much prosperity as the swan." Sometimes works of art produce captions instead of images ——— captions to experience, real or imaginary. But this emphasis on experience is perhaps a very American emphasis. The young French scholar Chloé Thomas said as much to me just the day before yesterday. Americans value both the gaining of experience and the having of experiences, and access to experience is a prominent element in America's narrative of itself ———its self-consciousness. Hence its obsession with geography (as a medium for experience as well as for expressive, physical, and economic freedom), and its insistence on human beings as agents of history and culture (so that they "make something happen"). And so a character in a narrative comes along, a protagonist, in variable, quotidian disguise. I cannot speak to the experiences that are had by a stone (say of rain or sunlight falling on its surface, or a sow bug crawling under it), or a nasturtium (say of an ant's feet on one of its petals, or water rising through a stem), nor even, with any confidence, by my long-haired white and orange cat with the large fluffy tail, but for humans, every experience elicits other experience. That's what experiencing for humans is: an amplification and intensification of our sense of ourselves amidst other presences in the world. In this sense, every experience is symbolic, the evocation and provocation of meaning, which is itself experienced. Say I fall in love, or aspire to an intensity of friendship with another, so as to participate in the workings of his or her mind. I want to see all the sites he or she finds exciting, the places he or she is now planning to revisit. I feel a vague anxiety, however, since doing so will take up a lot of my time, and maybe, in any case, I'm not invited. After the rainy night, there comes a pale morning, amorphous pale blue patches appear in the sky that seems nonetheless to have given up any attempt to cast daylight. He or she with whom I seek an intensity of friendship, a multi-layered history of shared experience, is driving and, without explanation (but I know that he or she has suddenly spotted something of interest, or that we've reached a destination), pulls off to the side of the road. I scan the terrain. From beyond the hum of the engine, through the open car windows, I hear the singing of birds in the trees and I'm frightened, knowing that they are not singing voluntarily, not claiming branches or giving an alert or flirting; they are spellbound, possessed. But everything that happens justifies the constant detecting of a constant detective. The detective I call Roy Robinson Trelaine has a maimed left hand and weeps in his sleep ———— "from boredom," he says. His theme seems to be that of distrust or ambivalence or "the unbearable realism of a dream." Hearing a dubious opinion, Roy Robinson Trelaine responds with caution or frustration or with a sense of overwhelming sleepiness. Finding that something lacks plausibility, veracity, credibility, reality, I too lose interest. I resent the waste of my time, energy, attention. Sufficiently bored, I grow hostile. Perhaps boredom, like pain, can be quantified; on a scale of 1 to 10, how bored are you? By the time one's level of boredom is approaching 10, it's ceasing to be boredom and becoming panic, or rage, an excess of feeling, a counter to boredom, but worse.

23

As the sun rises, breezes blow. But the sun doesn't "rise." Duh, says Jonah Giacomo Martin. The effects of a given time and place are in play. Daily life is underway, under the texture, timbre, surface of contexts. Historical realities are constantly rearranging overlapping finitudes. Things get imbricated and it is in their shifting configurations that they create history's terrain. It is a continuum, but in continuity's most fragile and momentary condition. And I in my dream am furious at a neighbor whose lions have escaped. She has climbed into her yellow Volkswagen, she starts the engine and looks into the rearview mirror to check behind the car. In the small, intricate, and brightly colored painting framed in the mirror, she recognizes herself, minute as a bumblebee. Microcosms, like eternities, offer vast potential for concrete and specific realities, in which even a woman's or man's or domestic cat's or snapdragon's most fantastical imaginings and most extraordinary hallucinations are included. When imagining intelligences in relation to wholes, I imagine them gathering together fragments, shards, pieces, bits and uniting them into intelligibility. But surely I don't think that imaginations simply assemble puzzle pieces into pictures. Along with scraps of matter, assemblages of actuality include elements of affect, the realia of allegory, emitting imaginative addenda from the facts at hand. This is very close to the philosophic method as Alfred North Whitehead conceives of it. "The success of the imaginative experiment is always to be tested by the applicability of its results beyond the restricted locus from which it originated." The frightened withdraw behind the curtain of their fear, but, unlike the fierce student activist Paco David Fantine, they don't become more honest with themselves within the privacy they insert themselves into. Paco David Fantine is like an old person in his honesty, his objectivity. "We will persuade stubborn facts to become less stubborn," he says. The aggression associated with the avant-garde —— its iconoclastic or agonistic relation to the dominant society ——is real; through its oppositional activities, the avant-garde struggles to bring about the epistemological break necessary for destabilizing people's assumptions and generating cognitive uncertainty and cultural porosity. But that's only the first phase of avant-garde practice, the prelude to its real task, which is to forge new social as well as cognitive connections, to generate new forms of connectivity, and to deepen as well as expand membership in the world of interconnectedness, such that the sphere of awareness and care is, so to speak, internatural as well as inter-racial and international —— and never universalist. At times the muses of sweeping, in league with the muses of counting, take possession of the bourgeois homeowner fervently practicing domestication. One sweep, two sweeps, ten sweeps, and soon she or he has swept one hundred sweeps and the leaves that were resting on the steps between front door and street have been swept away. Motes of November sunlight drift overhead on the summer dust turning in the air. They disappear into the shadow of the building, where the air is suddenly cooler. The contrast is palpable, a matter not just of temperature but of mood and duration, affect and instant. There are people who feel they live because they are wanted, desired, have been given or have acquired purpose or value. And there are others who feel they live by chance, at random, outside explanation, without justification. Jurors are released —— Samuel Wang Xie, Marisa Emily Wetherington, Lyn Hejinian, and the others —— since inventing them, and inserting them into this essay, I've let them go their various ways. Now Judge Lorna Kelly Cole of the criminal court appears at the top of the courthouse stairs in her electric wheelchair. Mechanical legs emerge from the sides of the chair, complete with plastic feet. The left leg stretches forward, settles a foot on the first concrete courthouse step, the chair lifts slightly, the right foot joins the left. The judge in her chair descends the stairs. For a moment, when she reaches the sidewalk, it looks as if she'll fall backwards, but she rights herself with a bounce, the mechanical legs retract, Judge Lorna Kelly Cole rolls almost regally northward along the sidewalk, a brown canvas briefcase on her lap. She is said to be "a woman of great courage." Let's say that improvement of the human mind is the goal of art —— but to do so assumes that human minds are in need of improvement. That's probably the case. But what's wrong with them? What and how are human minds lacking, deficient, wrong, malfunctioning, inadequate, faulty, etc. And what can art do, being a human undertaking, to instruct or excite improvement? And what would this improved human mind think, imagine, or experience, apart from increased pleasure and increased pain. It matters ———at least, it matters to me ——— that the happening of anything is experienced as the happening of something. The trunk of the redwood tree experiences the scampering of two squirrels up and down its trunk. The highway experiences the mobile pressure of each passing car. My white and orange cat experiences the strokes of my right forefinger just behind the right side of his jaw. Reality, whatever that is, doesn't miss any of this, and whether or not we miss it probably doesn't pertain to the future of reality. The orientation of the temporal past is horizontal; it reaches into the distance. The orientation of the psychological past is vertical; it sinks downward, in search of memories. There, too, lies the fragmented future. In a classroom just off the plaza, a discussion of The Dubliners is underway. "James Joyce followed out the consequences of realism and all it got him was despair," says Charlie Altieri. That Altieri is delighted by this outcome ——— that he considers it the only creditable outcome of a realist attitude, the only real lesson that reality can deliver ——— is clear. He shrugs, smiles, shifts his weight. He resettles himself on the edge of a table at the front of the lecture hall. Despair may now have brought us back to realism.

> Let's do something
> with abandon
> abandoning something
> as we go
> as we can't help but go
> and do so
> viewing something we see with abandon.

Doing is highly thought of and frequently abandoned.

Here it is, the gush of water from the tap. Well ——— there it was. I will not pretend to be writing this beside the kitchen sink. Past events can recur, and sometimes do, but for different reasons each time, and with different results. I'm writing at my desk, but before saying so I looked up, away from the keyboard and computer screen, as if to locate myself ——— or, rather, to orient myself in relation to the branches of the trees overhanging the small backyard and the stretch of worktable to my left and right. One of the squirrels is chattering angrily, aggressively, defensively (but I can't know its mood or feelings) from somewhere in the redwood tree at the edge of the neighbor's yard ——— not interrupting my thoughts but admitting unrelated sensation to them, adding small perceptions, contributing the contrasts, however slight, that mark the present moment as what it is, and as where I am. But when it is the universe that turns its phenomenological face to us, we usually can't read it. In a secular world, improbability is a source of excitement, even of what one might term spiritual excitement, which is to say wonder. The improbable is simultaneously a particular and limitless. Something like a chemical or electric charge surges into existence at the point at which incompatible perspectives collide. A flash of history, illuminating a bit of landscape, gets intensified by almost trivial circumstances. Paco David Fantine is nervous, a condition he betrays through an excessive display of profound empathic engagement with everything and anything he encounters. He says to Maggie Fornetti, "You're awesome." He repeatedly rubs his forehead. Anxiety-ridden flattery principally conveys anxiety. His face appears slightly impassive but wary, as if it were a cat he is absentmindedly caressing. A permanent sense of permanent alterity is the precursor to a mental life, a psychic life, an inner life. I can't help but like Paco David Fantine. Svetlana Alpers tells us (in The Art of Describing) that "early on the morning of 5 August 1676 just before, as we know from his diary, Constantijn Huygens the Younger was to start the search for the body of his great nephew, killed the day before in battle, he settled down with pen, ink, and paper to describe the besieged city of Maastricht viewed across the river Meuse." The result is a stark but exquisite drawing, suffused with loneliness. The miniaturized city, distanced by war as well as geography, is visible across a stretch of smudged, rather than ruffled, water. Almost filling the drawing's foreground are two boats, partially hidden behind some bushes that stand between us and the dock at which they are tied. The air is almost still —————— the pennants hanging from the masts of the boats barely flutter, and the sail on a boat visible to the right on the scarcely moving Meuse is luffing. The stillness is a product of tension, not of calm. The atmosphere is forlorn, the moment beset by personal and political sorrow. The activist remains dependent on the capitalist powers against which she protests; she is capitalism's second meaning ————— the meaning that her actions, always allegorical, release into view. A bird, a common house sparrow, is flitting between branches of the street trees ————— ash, purple leaf plum, unpruned sycamores ————— while above three gulls fly a jagged route that more or less follows the 51B bus line south from the university campus to Broadway, crossing from one city into another, the first so closely allied in the public imagination with its university (with a force that UCLA, for example, could never exert on Los Angeles) as to seem a city of intelligent youth and radical, if not new, ideas, and the second so frequently berated for its non-renewable "downtown" and ineradicable grit and malaise as to seem a city of both difficulty and inconsequence ————— a city at once inadequately and excessively urban. As Norbert Guterman and Henri Lefebvre note (in La Conscience mystifiée, from which Walter Benjamin quotes in The Arcades Project), "[W]e should investigate the underside of all sincerity." They go on, with some sarcasm: "But bourgeois culture and democracy are too greatly in need of this value! The democrat is a man who wears his heart on his sleeve; his heart is an excuse, a testimonial, a subterfuge. He is professionally heartwarming, so he can dispense with being truthful." Generosity and compassion, too, have an underside. As does happiness. So I've come to it now. One of the kids who's been hanging out at the Oakland MAP has been killed on an Oakland street corner. Or somewhere in the turbulence of a political demonstration. In either case, he was only a bystander, now relegated to the lists of collateral damage. Askari Nate Martin is talking to his mother. I don't want to identify his mother. I don't want to know which of my characters it is. I dreamed

him up, created him, imagined his shirt, his black hair, his ges-
tures ———— the way he would sweep his right hand in a small
circle for emphasis when he spoke, as if passing a small ball
through the air. Now as I write this I contribute to the event of
his death, its scene, its time, its spread. I swell with an equiva-
lent of anger, anxiety, guilt. I suffer from the desire to improve.
Lucretius, writing on animal affect, says, "Heat is the element
that predominates in those creatures whose hearts are fierce
and whose irascible minds readily seethe with anger. First and
foremost in this class are lions, so strong and ferocious: often
they growl and roar until they burst their bellies, since they are
unable to repress their tempestuous rage. On the other hand,
the chill minds of deer contain more wind and are quicker to
send icy currents of air blowing through the flesh, thus inducing
a trembling motion in the limbs." There are times when dream-
ing thrusts me into phantasmagorical mortality ———— anguish,
anger, excess, the most extreme forms of memory. Thinking
forgets to intercede, fails to interpret. Or when it does, it gen-
erates disenchanted allegories, allegories of disenchantment,
allegories of the impossibility of allegory. "There's a sermon
now, writ in high heaven, and the sun goes through it every
year, and yet comes out of it all alive and hearty." For most of
the period I've been working on this book, its title has been
The Positions of the Sun. Bodies emerge out of an anarchic iri-
descent flutter. Shadows can't shrink from them. But it might
have been called Wild Captioning. Eloise Steve and Rachel
Butter meet at a café. They spot an empty table and Eloise
Steve drops her scarf on it, Rachel Butter puts a book on it. They
go to the counter to order. For Eloise Steve a chai, for Rachel
Butter an espresso, they agree to share a macaroon, "for here
or to go?" asks the counter man, "for here" they say in chorus,
"por aquí" he says to his side kick the barista, "gracias," says
Rachel Butter, mispronouncing the word. Things happen, cap-
tions accrue. "Nothing can be added to history other than one's
awareness of it." We can only caption that.

24

In whatever one does, one deploys or proffers or expresses or articulates or displays both conscious and unconscious style. Or we could call it esprit, and that might entail panache, éclat, or, antithetically, despondency, dysphoria, ire. To the degree that one's style (or styling) is conscious, it's an expression not just of one's attitudes but of who one thinks one is or wants to be or wants to be believed to be. It's more than adjectival or predicative; it's self-definitive, a mode of transit. To the degree that it's unconscious, so-called natural, or, rather, to the degree to which, as far as oneself is concerned, it's formative (constitutive of how one is, the determination of one's manner) —— it's adverbial. And also probably predictable. Either way, one adopts style on behalf of its survival value. It provides one with a way to practice overcoming something, even perhaps oneself, or the moods that seem identical with oneself, self-determining. The idiom that describes one as "retreating into one's interiority" misrepresents the situation. Introspection is not a retreat; it's an advent, into an unquiet space, generally gloomy, certainly not restful. We are not talking about oblivion here, nor safety, nor domesticity, nor the familiar; interiority is much more likely to present one with troubles. Among the more mild of them are doubt and ambivalence, since they are indigenous to interiority, which is, after all, an arena for muddling. Through style, the deployment of our adopted syntax, we (humans) forge connections. Connectivity is the advantage humans have over happenstance. Weak as we are, it's our principal instrument of defense. We develop syntax, take on style, so as to prevail. Without the network of connections that result, we, as solitary individuals, are pathetic, innocuous, blank, weak, incapable of defending or even taking care of ourselves. Style allows us to link ourselves, even if negatively, to other beings. Grammars —— by which I mean all kinds of connecting tactics —— are our instruments of invention, as well as of power. But they are only a crutch. Having a capacity for grammar hardly justifies our thinking we have mastered the world. Time goes by. The funeral for the dead boy is over. It's almost December. It's dark, very late, a man is passing slowly through the neighborhood. He pushes a grocery cart, the bottles and cans in it clink and clatter. He sings something, a short refrain, hardly more than a mumbled melody ———— or memory ———— embedded in his voice. As he sings, he gains something: weeping ———— he weeps. A flash of pathos. Yes! But freedom is always qualified ———— dedicated, flaunted, overseen, negated. The gravitational force of weeping pulls at one's inner world, from which it picks up scraps of the past. The gravitational force of the happy imagination pulls at the outer world, dragging material into perception. Askari Nate Martin sighs in his sleep, and Maggie Fornetti feels his breath on her face before she realizes she's heard it. His breath is slightly stale; she turns over, the comment "I'm changing my olfactory orientation" crosses her mind and amuses her, and she falls back to sleep. Freedom lies in dreams. Somewhere non-freedom lies, too. Cretaceous thimbles, metal delectables, sporadic blankets, and effigies en croute? I must think of myself as a plaything of chance, a product of contingency. I remain still largely indeterminate, incompletely formed, despite my being now over 70. I'm subject to the weather, to aging, to gravity, to thirst. I'm subject to myriad objects. Here are some of the many useful instruments of a late November day around the Thursday of Thanksgiving: baster, bed, belt, blanket, book, boots, bra, bread board, broom, bus, candlestick, carving knife, cash, cell phone, chair, Clingwrap, coat, coffee maker, colander, comb, computer, deodorant, desk, dishwasher, doorknob, dust pan, envelope, faucet, file folder, garbage can, glass, glasses, gravy boat, hairbrush, hair dryer, hand lotion, jar, key, knife, mouse, mug, notebook, paper, pen, pencil, pie dish, pillow, plate, platter, postage stamp, pot, printer, radio, rake, refrigerator, roasting pan, rolling pin, shampoo, shirt, shower, sink, skillet, skirt, soap, socks, sofa, spatula, sponge, spoon, stapler, stove, sweater, table, toaster, toilet, toothbrush, towel, umbrella, underpants, waste basket, watch, wine glass. Interrelated objects, producing occasions and prompting responses, can assemble into riddles. As such, their functional identity is in abeyance; who knows what's possible. Indeed, who knows what's happening, what has already happened? "If you abolish the whole, you abolish its parts; and if you abolish any part then that whole is abolished." What am I? Riddles proffer objects, situations, or images, but their identity is withheld. Memory has to cast about, so as to establish a connection with fate. And even then, though riddles arrange the sensible, they withhold the sense:

>A birch tree with ideas
>Freedom as gravel on a private road
>A melancholy admiral

The pleasure we feel when we get the riddle's answer is only partially intellectual. The real pleasure comes from the illusion of restored order. Dispersed parts are reunited into their apparent whole. Allegories, on the other hand, are not made out of parts, and the captioning of an allegorical image or situation activates what was in abeyance, latent, dormant ——— but not fragmented. "The stars have […] virtue for the allegorist: they belong in constellations. They are known from the earliest times to move in a strictly ordered system of mutually dependent relations." Dawn is not far off. The stars are fading. Maggie Fornetti is asleep on her side, right leg straight, left leg bent and drawn close to her body, left arm across her chest, right bent and tucked close to her side. Askari Nate Martin is asleep on his back, arms folded, legs straight, toes pushing at the bedding at the end of the bed. Loss and forgetting are intimately bound to the affective life of married love, with its intricate temporality, its persistent (though sometimes hard-won) lack of closure. In the course of a day, through the myriad small temporal increments, power relations in the domestic sphere shift, fading only temporarily as everyone sleeps. One night, I dream thirty words. Or I hallucinate them (they have the convincing force of perceptual truth when it grabs reality and won't let go) and see:

>a pronoun dog along, an adverb on
>the space and seam and purple is
>for every idiocy perfection of the abstract sea
>in rectangles of unaffiliated violet
>or pink vivacity

I'm not responsible for the words, they just show up in the dream. But they become my responsibility. I am tasked with situating them, placing them. And to do that I have to recognize the "units" into which they should be grouped. "Endlessly" ——— that's how I characterize my effort in the dream ——— endlessly, I "phrase." I have to pace and place the semantic arrival of the words, their "meaning units." But I'm not sure where to insert divisions. Selection requires decision, but (in the dream) indecision is what makes the phrases vivid. Indecision leaves intact the power of hallucinated particularity. I come to no conclusion. Waking, I quickly write the dream words, lineating as I do so, increasingly uncertain that what I'm writing down are actually the words that came to me, displayed on the dream screen. Waking solves nothing ——— quite the opposite. There's no epiphany. Of course not. Epiphanies negate particularity. Something ordinary and everyday, just as much as something outrageous or surprising, can be transformed into an aesthetic event, undergo an aesthetic realization, but it does so precisely by remaining particular. Still, it's difficult to resist the pull of seductive totality, which even the particular can exert. As, for example, in minimalist painting ——— and, perhaps, more problematically, in minimalist musical compositions, whose micro-modulations can become as pervasive as dust. The music may be luscious, and its intentions may be innocuous, while the effects are insidious, producing the mollifying effect of an all-encompassing ideology. As such, the performances of it become an elaborate advertisement for something that its listeners can't name but begin to long for ——— something that constrains their freedom, even as their minds wander. Traveling (which is by no means always a manifestation of freedom) seems to remove one from everyday life (demanding repetition). And yet, one of the great pleasures for a visitor comes from gaining competency in the everyday life (free-ranging repetition) of the strange, new, foreign place he or she is visiting ——— discovering where and how to get groceries, mastering the public transportation system, figuring out how to use the bathing and toilet facilities, etc. Pleasures? Those pleasured visitors, reveling in their competency, are probable tourists, business people, politicians, entrepreneurs. But there are exiles there too, expert at exile, old hands at getting by. Roy Robinson Trelaine has a raw blister on his right foot and this may be what's preventing him from moving swiftly forward again into the battle (his term), which, however, hasn't yet begun. With the pain, such as it is, comes a flicker of history. A spasm of memory ———— physical, physiological, geographic, and seemingly perpetual. The refugees, exiles, fugitives, or the merely stranded, confused, lost, or even, often, merely homesick ———— they suffer nausea, loss of appetite, agoraphobia. Much of everyday life in the nineteenth century took place in interiors ———— in the domestic sphere. In the twentieth century, it moved increasingly into the streets, at least in cities. In the twenty-first century everyday life has moved again, onto screens. At CAFÉ ROMA, Alice Milligan Webster and Judge Lorna Kelly Cole are sharing a convivial moment of misanthropy. Gears mesh, systems circle. In an essay on circuits and screens, capitalism's inventiveness is acknowledged, along with the complexities of its flow, over filigrees, planes, and curls. Gates swing with creativity, familiarity exerts creative sway. Two children, neither more than five or six years old, are running at pigeons on the sidewalk outside the café. The children are wielding wooden sticks like swords, jabbing at the pigeons, shrieking. Bulky, awkward, stupid, the pigeons, entirely without merriment, stay just out of reach. Here perhaps we can note "the power of nature," a subtle version of nature's destructive capacity: the tumult of storms, the geological upheavals of earthquakes and volcanoes, etc. We animalize them, so that we can turn them loose, unleashed, except in the case of drought, an ongoing devastating nonevent. The clouds refuse to release rain. Representations tend toward the metaphorical when they monumentalize. Memory presents itself conceptually as something very like nature, as all one thing, largely contingent, autonomously rational, with cycles of recurrence that are never the same. Like nature (at least until humans mucked with it so mercilessly that it became unnatural out of sheer self-defense), memory is self-stabilizing, but only because time is on its side. Elation gives way to calm, grief to acceptance or the lassitude of depression. The sky is the most standard blue. The blue everywhere is sky. When will it rain?

25

An irate young woman at the back of the room challenges me: "Why don't you write in some other language? All your writing is in English, the language of capitalism and imperialism!" I take her question more seriously than I should. Winter sunlight like a vague cold boulder fills the room, casting an asthmatic chill and leaving useless, gasping spaces between its surfaces and the walls. I can't say that the English language is always and everywhere blameless, I can't say that it's as neutral as a sculptor's block of marble (marble never comes neutrally to a sculptor). What are we to language or language to us? I couple pedantic with supermarket muzak, perpendicular with email. The woman is no more than thirty. She's white and has cornrowed her hair. As I'm responding to her challenge ——— looking at her, neglecting the themes and topics I've been invited to speak about so as to address her question, and becoming increasingly aware that the others in the room consider it silly ——— I'm suddenly furious, at myself. A man's name echoes back from a dream ——— Anton? Eugene? It's not in dreams but after them that I find myself beset by narcissistic self-loathing and embarrassment. The emotions flowing from ineffectuality, misplaced dutifulness, and frustration are as different from activist affect as melancholy is from excitement, anger from animal energy. But then one early morning to delight to dare in the rocking of a pine silhouetted against a pale plain sky just as the sunlight from below begins to bring out the glow of its mid-December old foliage when it could merely all be my own nodding becomes irrevocable. We can adventure bare-backed. Between a rider proudly controlling a horse and a rider sloppily galloping, two stories are underway, and sooner or later they will encounter each other. As for myself, if I weren't so light-complexioned that I'm virtually allergic to the sun, I would lie in the grass like a melon come summer, growing incrementally sweeter and sweeter. In time, the emotions of this melon (its cucurbitaceous or melopeponal affect) would be applied practically, the sweetness conveyed. In this temperate zone and always under human attack the winter colors are ochre and olive, sage and forest green, sere, impartial, and in abeyance. I remember more of the dream, or suddenly, perhaps, at such high speed that I'm unaware of the process, I dream it now into memory. An elderly man ———— he is Anton or Eugene ———— loves me passionately, and is innocently joyous to be loved in return by such a young and beautiful woman as I. What a relief. As with all dreams, the as effect is in play, rendering me, who was earlier furious, "young and beautiful." Love is not an emotion but a condition beset by unresolvable contradictions. I am often rendered hypocritical by them. From sheer joy we run down the hill, a large protesting crowd, with me in the front, having flung my banner aside. My old lover is behind me, struggling; in the back of my mind there lurks a faint concern for him and then growing irritation that he can't, or won't, keep up. The sun moves softly over much of the scene, but it is intensifying the rest. Our pace slows and becomes routine, we alter our route awkwardly. We need to hesitate but can't, since now we concentrate our full attention on our goal ———— a cluster of blind buildings. We take our proper private and public bodies toward them. Memory can't even begin to recreate those bodies, and description can't experience them. Memory-informed knowledge is fallible, but at least it sustains historical consciousness. It is quite different from the omniscience of an ahistorical, or history-obliterating, God. Imagining deity as exempt from history is one of the many failings of monotheism. Here: to illustrate what I mean by "a flash of history," let me remind you of the fable known as "Two Riders, a Bundle, and a Monetary Exchange." As it unfolds, an unlikely intersection of different occurrences takes place, producing an event, and this event enriches a young man purely by chance. And all the while it remains inexplicable. As is the case with so much of what happens by chance, nothing can account here for the fact that a tight-reining equestrian on an arch-necked black horse drops a bundle of cash inadvertently from his pocket directly onto the spot where a novice on a bad-tempered pony lands an hour later when he is bucked off. The novice finds his head resting on the bundle, lifts his head, sees the cash, and picks it and then himself up. A week goes by but the novice can't find the money's previous owner, so he takes it to share with family and friends, whose gratitude over the following years makes him a powerful —— and, better, a complete —— man. Maggie Fornetti turns to Askari Nate Martin and asks him to tell her again what he thought of her in their "circus days." He laughs. There can hardly be a "complete life" without the experience of friendship and the excitement of camaraderie. They converge with the patterns formed by one's habits, or the habits —— the ways —— of one's public and private life, to form the backdrop against which one's memories play and out of which new ones form. Neither the networks of friendship nor the tapestry of ways are always legible, even to oneself. And at multiple points, for no apparent reason, encounters or happenstance or incoming circumstances and particulars alter them. Whole worlds can come down to a way, or depart from one. "In those days" (whenever and whatever they were) "I used often to..." seeks to evoke abandoned, superseded, or lost ways, or to establish as reality things that scarcely existed. Those days belong as much to stories as to history: appearance of the world, disappearance of coherence. If no ideas in the Platonic sense exist, if there are no eternal forms —— if reality is devoid of them —— , then is allegory even possible? Perhaps the best, unidealized (particular and local) meanings we can produce appear in comedy; or, perhaps, in social life. There the inherence of the element of pathos would be self-evident. In this context, the sun is a strange particular, and something's death is another. "Death does not destroy things so completely that it annihilates the constituent elements [of a being]: it merely dissolves their union. Then it joins them in fresh combinations and so causes all things to alter their forms and change their colors, to acquire sensation and resign it in an instant." In saying this, Lucretius seems to suggest that death is a creative power, an engine of processes, a genius of reconfiguration and reconstitution. He was writing in an age when people dared to fear death, or dared to not fear it. Cyclical time, like cyclical processes (the sprouting of a tree from the rotting of a pear), was everywhere evident. Linear time was still waiting for humanity's leap into it. Is that the way we achieved our separation from nature? There is probably no other creature capable of conceiving of the irrevocable. I know that Tad Magee was raised by a mean-spirited, resentful, vituperative mother and that he is perpetually beset by an insatiable yearning to be loved. To a great extent, I invented him. From a young age he has worked excessively hard, largely in an effort to please people; now in his late fifties, he has become a philanthropist ——— or, as his angry daughter Tamarind puts it, a fucking hypocritical, impotent do-gooder. Tad Magee has history, but it shows no necessary connection between the mother of Tad Magee and his philanthropy, nor between her grandmother and Tamarind Magee's current delinquency. No chronological account can explain the production of character. Likewise, an account of the production of knowledge will always fail to explain certain kinds of learning and the conditions that excite it. The happy life has its multiple sources of satisfaction, its many things to be interested in. But they seem very often to be precluded from the life of the exhausted, the depressed, the driven, the defeated. The afternoon light is thinning as pale sheets of cloud drift overhead. At the moment, young Rosario Basho Clark is drawing, as he does almost obsessively, regardless of the occasion. He seems not to care <u>what</u> he draws so much as <u>that</u> he is drawing, albeit always in relation to what he sees or remembers seeing ——— as if visibility itself were presenting his eyes and hands (he's ambidextrous) with its compelling challenge, reminding him that he is coexistent with reality (there), and with a body (here) ——— presented, that is, with a complex quandary, the reality of his presence in reality. Outside, Rosario Basho Clark suddenly looks up, touches his incipient goatee, and smiles at Sophie-Anne Solander. Subjectivity is a product ——— a construct ——— not of consciousness but of the consciousness of consciousness. Consciousness of consciousness is what separates the experiencing subject from the world of objects that he or she is experiencing. Ok ——— but that separation is short-lived. "Tacit knowing is built up over time; it is cumulative, not because it piles new information on top of former information, but because it builds the new into the old, and thus makes experience denser" ——— a passage that struck me, when I encountered it, as speaking directly to the capacity of the quotidian to provide experience with particularity and difficulty. In this respect it evades the categorical (in whatever manifestation it takes, including that of nation or nationality), which establishes and maintains itself on the rational principle of unification. Categorical knowledge insists on homogeneity (and, in the social sphere, unanimity, or, at least, a pretense of commonality). The processes of knowledge that produce it are never contemplative; rather, in being procedural, they involve alteration, reduction, suppression. Real heterogeneity can best be encountered when lingering. I am reminded of a conversation with Larry Eigner's brother Richard, who wondered aloud whether Larry Eigner, in writing Through, Plain, his (still unpublished) novella about the disordering experiences of a disabled young man at a summer camp, had been influenced by Proust. Richard supposed (I don't know why) that it was unlikely that Larry had read all of À la recherche, but, he said, given Larry's habit of "mulling things over," even a small amount of input tended to make a powerful impression on him. Every work of art sets some standards, however idiosyncratic (or undisclosed) they might be. These are not standards by which things can be tested for their reality. It is something else in things that a work of art tests —————— their vitality? their solicitation of our strange participation? their purveying of encounter? their capacity to move us? or simply to move? Larry Eigner's novella ends abruptly, mid-sentence, with

some question or as if some question what to do

That's it; whatever more might have been said remains in abeyance.

26

I am not a bra, nor a thriving coastal pine tree, nor a voyage; I am still ambivalent. One can't mete out wholeness; children don't do so and the old shouldn't either. Wholeness is loose and temporary ——— a kind of fog. Still I'm capable of serious appreciation ——— but that could also be said of a chump or insecure fool as well as of an advocate or empiricist. Perhaps it's cowardly to appreciate. Montaigne says that <u>sadness</u> is characteristic of cowardice; he also calls it (in "Of Sadness") "a stupid and monstrous ornament." Nonetheless, it is an unavoidable part of anything on which ornamentation might appear. The Christmas tree, for example, or the tagged walls of warehouses and loft spaces along Oakland's waterfront. Crews of graffiti-removers paint the ornamentation out, effacing sadness. Bone! F that. Going about her daily life on a side street west of College Avenue, Ellie North Roth is thinking these days about night life daily and daily life every night, as old age weaves them together, into something thicker and thicker, worn thinner and thinner. There are food chains, queen bees, trauma centers, sidecars, tangos, a white and orange longhaired cat, several days at last of melodious winter rain. These, accumulating, diverging ——— they contribute to subjectivity, strengthen a person's individuation. In the quest for heterogeneity, for everything myriad, multiple, and different, one has to look outside of oneself, counter-introspectively. Even a writer of so-called lyric poetry should be disputing the validity of long-standing models of literary writing as introspective or retrospective. For reasons not exclusively his own, Askari Nate Martin rarely states what he loves, nor that he loves. Everyone is waiting, he says. Some fight while they wait, some share in the waiting. Pertinence, relevance ——— a constellating magnetic force of attraction ——— may intrude at any point and from any place, sourceless as time (though not otherwise resembling time). "No chain is homogeneous: all of them resemble, rather, a succession of characters from different alphabets in which an ideogram, a pictogram, a tiny image of an elephant passing by, or a rising sun may suddenly make its appearance." Misanthropes and philanthropists alike wait for a green light. An old woman fumbles with her coin purse at a supermarket checkout counter. Two students, sheltered from the rain by the overhanging awning of a shoe shop, interact intently with whatever's appearing on their cell phone screens while they wait for the bus. Art is capable of holding together assemblages very different from the ones that we think are credible, or probable, or that we think we can know. Coming in from the rain, Willem takes off his cycling gloves, Bill removes his shoes. Episodes of turbulence erupt out of the pull of everyday life, even out of the pull of domesticity ———— the call to breakfast, to the phone, to the kitchen for an English muffin spread with goat cheese or marmalade or for scrambled eggs and a Kellogg's Pop Tart®, to bed, and perhaps to sex. To politicize people's responses to such calls we could begin by asking how freely they answer. Don't want to mistake free fall for free flow. One doesn't make progress in the living of everyday life (facing repetition), except insofar as growing up, aging, declining, and dying can be construed as progress. Can it? Hardly. Every city emits its peculiar spatiality as an expression of its conditions. Dude! Rosario Basho Clark nods. It's chill, he says. Yeah? says Flip. He's momentarily frozen in fascination at the fact that swirling and vibrating and spinning atoms are the true reality of a table or bedroom wall. Everything that's holding together may cease to do so. Flip raises his right arm. That's it! It's all percussion! Things don't go into memory they emerge out of it. The friend they called Commando was once very much somewhere and then suddenly everywhere. Ellie North Roth lingers and awaits experience in the seemingly negative space of a rainy late afternoon of the holidays. To engage emptily in this way, in the art of abeyance, should bring one close to the non-particular, the unidentifiable, to all that is withheld because it is changing, she thinks. She attempts to let go of her place at the window; the changing makes her slightly afraid. She can refuse epiphany but she won't refuse weeping. Memory's inability to assemble wholes is one of its greatest virtues, Ellie North Roth says to Albert Sing Roth. I suppose, he says. Albert Sing Roth is a strong man, somewhat opinionated, but he's neither a bully, nor an ideologue, nor a martinet, nor a narcissist. If memory thinks it can foresee the future, it is generally deluded, he says. Along with the creation of the private worlds that aesthetic work draws us into, certainly art, or some of it at least, should create public worlds, as it used to, in much earlier times. It's possible that these public worlds might be as obsession-fraught or as dream-woven as private ones, or even that they would be unimaginable ———— bereft of images. In her introduction to <u>Becomings</u>, Elizabeth Grosz, writing on the threshold of a new millennium, speculates as to the character of possible futures and ends by wondering "whether this time of the future is the noble time of the lost cause, the time of an impossible future, in which one must struggle for, and achieve, a beyond in the most apparently hopeless and oppressed of positions." A few pages later she continues: "The politics of the hopeless cause, the cause ennobled precisely because it is hopeless, improbable, unlikely to succeed, introduces another [order of] time, another dimension, into the concept of what politics and struggle are. To struggle not to win so much as to make a mark, to mark a time and a place as particular, is to imbue time (and space) with a hope that is beyond the hope of actual outcomes." An inventive young poet wants to project into his forthcoming book some images from a large sheet of film, a 10 by 22 inch sheet of orange acetate with a "tongue" at one of the narrow sides just like the tongue used to thread a roll of 35mm film into a pre-digital camera. His girlfriend suggests that he make a cardboard mat with a round hole in it: the poet could slide the sheet so that the desired image would appear in the hole, backlit and thus projected. I say something like "that's a great idea"; it's a ridiculous thing to say. The poet's orange acetate sheet of film is creased and breaking apart. He says he is going to make a new one, but I don't trust the poet's sincerity. In a notebook I sketch an empty rectangle and write under it a caption: <u>a three alley dream whose interpretation requires a sword-swallower's practicality and an office on location so she or he can speak French to the money guys who have expectations that will remain forever unforgiven</u>. Unsatisfied, I try again, under a second empty rectangle: <u>At the scene of his true crime a killer</u>

checks his pockets, searching for his notes about weak feelings that will allow him to wade indifferently away from the gore at the sight of which passersby with enthusiasm will narcissistically express their own feelings, always their true object of fascination. This is better, but for the fun of it I dream up another. I draw a third empty rectangle and below it carefully write From between two dark high-rises a car, so blindingly white as to constitute a speeding site of pure negativity, comes into view and further accelerates, bearing down on a sunny round yellow car which it smashes, catapulting it into the side of a rose red car in Kirk Wong's 'Crime Story,' which we can take to mean that betterment will be as it always has been: littered with broken machines. I have no idea what might go into the empty rectangles. An epic is a long story about the difficulties that impede someone's attempt to return home. The hero's persistence is the real substance of his or her heroism. The kids at the Oakland MAP are searching for a proper place for themselves, a world with a horizon. They have predators: dealers, gang-bangers, bacteria, guns, cars, viruses, cops, idiots ———— general malignity. For humans alive in any given age, various ideas dominate as to the value of life, or the value of what's available (or not) to the living, and each age has its accompanying array of hobbies, culinary preferences, and child-rearing practices. Some ages ———— perhaps most ———— lose their canonical status; what they in their time thought constituted the value of life loses credibility, or even reality. Other ages accumulate value, becoming valuable in their own right. The ages, here given in alphabetical order, include:

> The Avian Age
> The Age of Ends
> The Age of Façades
> The Feline Age
> The Age of Games
> The Age of Herpetology
> The Age of Immediacy
> The Age of Justification
> The Martial Age (aka the Age of War)
> The Martian Age (also known as the Age of Origins)

The Age of Meteorology (sometimes confused with
   the Avian Age; see above)
The Musical Age (with a period of harsh timbres and
   unmelodious atonality following a long period
   of harmony and preceding a period of rampant
   percussion)
The Ocular Age
The Age of Representation (aka the Age of Return)
The Age of Time (sometimes called the Age of Now)

"During the day I was sustained and inspirited by the hope of night: for in sleep I saw my friends, my wife, my beloved country...." Feverishly, Victor Frankenstein races across immense stretches of territory as he madly pursues his experiment and its destruction. His vast experiment was always driven by a particular form of homesickness. "Often [...] I persuaded myself that I was dreaming until night should come, and that I should then enjoy reality in the arms of my dearest friends." It is to reality that we turn when looking for the source, the cause, the realm of existence of those things that we think we can properly know. Such a reality ———— so-called "objective reality" ———— exists "over there," while we, the knowing (or not-knowing), move about restlessly over here, in exile. But now the very word itself is beginning to lose reality. So quickly we are already some days into winter and the strange aspirations that come with the rain. Much of the activism has moved indoors. The great accomplishment that coherence achieves, as in a painting by Bonnard, are its murky verges.

CODA

The quotidian is cast. From its plasticity I pull this butterflied paperclip using this tide-marked thumb. A neon-green street sweeper crosses the surface of the quotidian and passes a tattling car door. I step over a flyer in the gutter on a sheet of pink paper. Willy-nilly things from the smooth day contribute to us. There's no universal unit of perception or experience. Mood pursues mood. Contestations proliferate. "Each generation must discover its mission, fulfill it or betray it, in relative opacity." Say I believe in what I've done, what I do, but then am asked by some contemporary turbulent set of circumstances not to believe in any of it any more. But my willingness and even ability to entertain the not-believing in what I've done and do is an inherent part of what I've done and do, and I can't not believe in that. I refuse that unbelief ———— that one, at least. Simone de Beauvoir, remembering a period of political despair (her response to the brutal repression of the Algerian resistance to French colonial occupation), wrote, "I loathed it all ———— this country, myself, the whole world."

> O radar o'clock
> O thronging candidates for office, for orifice-n't
> O Marianne Andersen'd've and Frantz Fanon'd've
> Ne'er O just once we'll and I'm and you'd and they'll
> O herewith, therefore, foothills, afternoon'm
> O politicized apples'd
> O monetized watered've
> O rising prices've and falling leaves're
> O mottled uninformative skin and prerecorded news
> and podcast wind

Chronology is the science of living anxiously, the science of nervousness, perseveration, insomnia, sore feet. Or perhaps it's the site of immobility, or identity, or obligation, or loss, though not of rest or shared moments. Chronologists, being, most often, traditionalists and puritanical, organize grimly; their mythological prototypes are the Fates and the Furies. Time should be free of chronology ———— chronology is not the proper syntax of time. In a letter to a friend, Lady Mary Wortley Montagu asks, "Who are the most despicable creatures?" Immediately, she herself answers: "Certainly, Old women." Her next question and answer follow: "What pleasure can an old woman take? – Only Witchcraft." Lady Mary is over seventy and mocking herself, but I would bet that she's doing so with some sense of daring (rather than unease), since she's writing in 1758 and it was less than a quarter of a century since the passage of the Witchcraft Act of 1735 put an end to witch hunts in Great Britain. Iterations, quatrains, sessions of torture, carousels, maternity wards, swollen ankles, dark skin, festivals, empty breasts, cir- cuses ———— these belong to the syntax of time. Proper names, too. Pronouns, Avocadoes. And endgames, bringing whispers, rumors, echoes: take notice, no knot, no kiss, no account, and have no counter but encounter to continue. Rhymes provide pause and respite, or wit, or a false halt, exorcism, or satisfac- tion, or they produce a cringe, giggle, shrug, delight, disdain. With that: out of bed and into the daylight, strong foot on bare board. My defenses are on full alert, ready to fend off irritation, outrage, gutter, clatter, sadness. 7:23 am. Daily life is lived at times ———— epochal, instantaneous, remembered. Times abound with surreptitious superstitions. First days are frequent. But it's the task of a rational being to view things without the aspect of eternity. And any last day, like the annual last day, has its own kind of dailiness and quotidian finesse. Henri Lefebvre has said that everyday life should be a work of art. If so, let's imagine it as being followed by an exegesis that is hardly exe- getical at all; it does little or nothing to explain or gloss what has been lived, artfully or haphazardly or obliviously. There's no necessary corollary between facts and how they appear to us and our experience of them and whatever explanation of this we might come up with. At the same time, there isn't neces- sarily a difference between these either. A work of art is not necessarily more original or more authentic or more exciting or less exacting than explanations of it. We can improvise. We can be specific. Farts do not explain cabbage, lists do not explain decision, a sense of the absurd does not do away with sincerity. The point of exegesis is to dare to both make and break connections. Poetics (exegetical insofar as it offers an account of a method of making) is always also an erotics (an account of a given confirmation of desire), and every important poem is a grand manifestation of human frustration. Fate produces chances. As a result, we are faced with choices and make decisions. Exercising them leaves containment (including the inner sanctum of romantic introspection) in ruins. "If I stop to describe the present this present is already gone; I have already drowned in archaeology. I push the needle of the present just a little bit further, and find myself exactly where my desire, my smile, my certitude are. And I live my future immediately." Tonight Maggie Fornetti and Askari Nate Martin, as I imagine them, will have a party, serving a late dinner followed by the requisite lingering. In due course, noise and time will converge, even if only incompletely. 11:49 am: In the produce aisle, Maggie surveys the variegated greens, the almost floral display of lettuces: iceberg, romaine, butter, radicchio, endive, arugula, red leaf, mâché, frisee, a vignette of vegetables with flirtatious leaves, crinkled, crisp, succulent, curved, bitter, convex, ovate, spicy, frilled, sweet. Maggie Fornetti pulls back her hair, spins it around a finger, presses the coil to the back of her head, and secures it in place with a tortoiseshell barrette. Actions only take place in the present ——— this is obvious enough. And when attention is focused entirely on the present, completeness is impossible. One is bound to whatever comes to one's consciousness. That is a more or less adequate definition of our relation to fate. What comes to one's consciousness binds one to one's fate. It is thus that fate becomes linked to incipience and also to incompleteness ——— infinitude (which is not at all the same as universality). The limiting condition known as fate, and the limiting condition known as beginning, converge, and the limits cancel each other. Time is no longer decisive; it no longer can supply desire with meaning. "I cannot part without regret from the stick I have taken from the hedge as I passed; I look back after it when I have thrown it away; we had made friends." So saying, the narrator of Xavier de Maistre's A Nocturnal Expedition Around My Room reminisces. 1:15 pm: Dorothy Blythe Ward is hiking on a trail in the Berkeley hills expressly to be moved. She walks with the intention ———— or hope ———— of being stirred by aesthetic emotions. She delights in appearances. The sensations might be of the most banal kind ———— a thrill of bliss at the site of shadows tumbling over the ground under the trees and of a tattered spider's web catching the sunlight that filters through their leaves, etc. She peers at the dry carapace of a bug in the web. She is in thrall to the aesthetic enchantment of a certain kind of otherness, and finds insects in particular to be constantly compelling. As Nietzsche says, "We have to <u>learn to think differently</u> ———— in order at last, perhaps very late on, to attain even more: <u>to feel differently</u>." We could dance the night away: we could engage fully in aesthetic exertion ———— the exercising of our aesthetic abilities. Hips, belly, butt: they wouldn't be in the service of self-intensification, they needn't increase knowledge or awareness or sensibilities. They wouldn't be in the service of anything. Formality and informality are indistinguishable in someone who is charming and animated from head to toe. We could play in air. Like the Harmonians of Fourier's phalansteries, we could move from pleasure to pleasure, delighting in the swoosh of the mop across the kitchen floor, reveling in the crunch of celery between our audacious molars, quivering at the tidal constellations, euphoric as the sunlight disappears. 5:30 pm: "I didn't like the Mozart," says Lorna Kelly Cole, dropping her program into the trash can to the right of the concert hall door. "You're probably too old to like anything in C major," says Charlie Altieri, who slept through much of the Fourth String Quartet and yet has heard every note of it. In a café across the plaza, a group of activists is meeting to plan an action, it's but another in a long series of protests, the activists are dispirited, their number is diminishing, rumors of defection and accusations of treachery are circulating. "Maybe we should do something incomprehensible, something crazy," says Renny Ben Phillips, looking up from his laptop. "Like what?" Rafe Cohen-Johnson is prying the plastic lid off a tray of sushi. "I don't know ———— stage an alarm-out." "Which is...?" asks Sammy Christine Blake. "Setting off the fire alarms in every commercial building we can get into. We'll call it a dis-occupation." Imagination is under a compulsion to bring everything it can cull into the present tense. But it has the ability ———— sometimes ———— to drive everything altogether out. The imagination has the capacity to draw a blank. "Doubt at Midnight," says Bethany Becker. "Coleridge," she says. "Doubt performs its secret ministry," she adds. Bethany Becker is in a mood to giggle, she feels defiant, alienated, pissed off. Bethany Becker leaves the café. 8:37 pm: Hoa Mia Macintyre is hurrying to put away the dishes, fold the laundry, before going to hear the band at ETHIOPIQUITY and tomorrow start anew. The avant-garde artist has a double dream, that of changing society and that of changing aesthetic sensibility. To achieve these seldom entails the same or even similar things. Maybe every inch will fall, says Jean Day. And every inch remain, I reply. This is not the correct answer, it's pessimistic, but it seems okay. If we lived in constellations rather than on a planet we would think not in binaries but in multinaries, polynaries. According to the Gregorian calendar, the terrestrial year includes an "extra day." It is given over to revelry and regret. Musicians rally, a time ball falls. Midnight nears the gallery of allegories. Representations flash. "It's never disappointing, is it, kids," says Maggie Fornetti, who thinks it always is. The sky above is clear, the moon is in a phase. On some other side of the world the sun shines. There are many solar allegories ————

> Not in Utopia ———— [...]
> But in the very world which is the world
> Of all of us, the place in which, in the end,
> We find our happiness, or not at all [...].

AFTERWORD
The Writing of <u>Positions of the Sun</u>

<u>Positions of the Sun</u> developed over several years, in response to an interrelated sequence of experiences and interests. Composition began in mid-2009, when, using the 2008-09 "financial crisis" as justification, the then President of the University of California (Mark Yudof) declared that the university was in the throes of a budget crisis and that emergency measures were required. A number of staff members and campus workers were laid off, many faculty were required to take "furloughs," and much of the work previously undertaken by university employees (grounds and building maintenance, dining hall services, campus transportation, etc.) began to be outsourced. Student "fees" (soon re-termed, more accurately, "tuition") went up by 33%. In my view, then and now, what was underway was the beginning of a prolonged neoliberal event whereby capital extended its efforts at privatization into the world of public education. For the first time in its history, in the fall of 2009, graduate and undergraduate students, faculty, and members of the University of California's five labor unions formed an informal but highly active alliance, especially on the UC Berkeley campus. Under the simple name of the "Solidarity Alliance," it organized a number of protest actions. Many of these were undertaken with other East Bay protest entities; many were high profile events: rallies, marches, the take-over of the Port of Oakland, the blocking of a local freeway. And, in due course, a small but vibrant manifestation of Occupy was in place on the Berkeley campus: Occupy Cal.

Protest never exists in a steady state—nor should it. Energies wax and wane. Fragmentation and factionalization develop. At several points, police brutality intimidated large numbers of protest participants. The increased tuition put students into deeper debt and/or sent them off campus to part-time jobs (or forced them to give up their studies altogether). University staff were similarly affected; at one point, one of the unions issued a report stating that some 30% of university staff members also worked shifts at Walmart and similar companies. The percentage of university workers with third jobs was even higher.

As readers of <u>Positions of the Sun</u> will readily see, anti-privatization activism forms the backdrop to this....

This what?

Initially I thought I would write a sequence of interrelated prose poems, of no established length. I wanted to include material from diverse sources and to do so overtly, quoting and citing other texts; establishing intertextuality in this way, I intended the work to be mimetic of interconnectivity more generally. I wanted, too, to stay alert to ambient patterns and quotidian recurrences, less as backdrop than as a substantive presence. I made lists; I went looking for things to enter into the index of public and private spaces, ever altering under an ever-moving sun. I drew up a map of all the commercial enterprises along a one-block stretch in my neighborhood and noted when one or another of the shops closed, or was replaced, in the changing landscape of capital in proximity to a university. (Some of the commercial changes are almost comical; at present, the site of a former market specializing in Italian food goods that went bankrupt is now home to a market specializing in virtually identical Italian food goods. One wonders if, at least in this case, capital remains the same and only the name has changed.)

There are twenty-six sections to <u>Positions</u>. Well—twenty-seven, since there's a "Coda." Each section purportedly gives an account of two weeks of a year. The coda marks the year's turn.

Chronological organization, paratactic structure, attention to the "sentence" (as distinct from the "line")—just as these things interested me when I was writing <u>My Life</u> and <u>My Life in the Nineties</u>, they have done so again. I have never ceased to be fascinated by processes (random and/or determinative) of interconnection (including, now, those forged in the process of community/protest organizing). Linkage has taken on a political valence, both on the ground and as a means of understanding what comes (is coming) to pass, what the roots of it are, what is at stake.

In the fall of 2010, I taught the first iteration of a UC Berkeley English department grad seminar addressed to the interplay between the aesthetic (art) and the everyday. It was called "Postmodernism and the Writing of Everyday Life." Subsequent versions have been called "The Turn to Language and the Writing of Everyday Life" and "Allegories of Late Capitalism and the Writing of Everyday Life." For better or worse, scholarly investigations of (and literary writings about) everyday life for a long time were deemed a quintessentially, if not exclusively, feminist domain (despite the magnificent contributions by Fernand Braudel and others of the Annales School). But this seems a thing of the (recent) past; the students participating in these seminars have come from many different university departments and have gender-identified in diverse ways; all have taken the theory and practice of everyday life as an area of extreme importance. As the titles I contrived for these seminars suggest, I was positing everyday life as a social space and thus as a political space. In other words, political struggle and everyday life can (and sometimes have to) converge. Or so I argued, and still do.

As the first of the sections got written, I changed my characterization of the work. I lost interest in calling it "prose poetry"; doing so seemed misleading, a misinterpretation. I began to term it an essay, "an essay with characters." As an essay, it extends my engagement with various theories and diverse practices of everyday life, situating them in an imaginative zone, an activist domain that is both political and aesthetic. It is a populated experiment, a study—in the sense that Stefano Harney and Fred Moten elaborate in the long interview at the end of The Undercommons: Fugitive Planning & Black Study: "study is what you do with other people. It's talking and walking around with other people, working, dancing, suffering, some irreducible convergence of all three, held under the name of speculative practice" (110).

I have always felt a premonitory melancholy when I become alert to the movement of humans—the coming and going, approaching and passing, mostly of people who are and will remain total strangers to me and to each other. I can't help but feel the pathos of our efforts, despite (or perhaps because of) the frequently beautiful results. I haven't tried to capture that—that is not what Positions is "about." But the book does follow characters, through public and private spaces, in a place and time during a period of rising political consciousness.

There are around seventy characters in the book, many mentioned only once (and a few named in my notes but never appearing by name in the text). They exist in contexts: geo-spatial, social, quotidian, temporal; they share contexts, they contextualize each other. They (and I with them, in conjunc-tion with the various texts I was reading in the course of writing the book) are engaged in study. Many of them are modeled loosely on people I know—students, campus activists, neigh-bors, family members. Several are real. (Jean Day and Charles Altieri "play themselves"; both have read the manuscript and are willing to remain as they are in its pages; Lyn Hejinian is mentioned.) Some characters, including Maggie Fornetti, Askari Nate Martin, and Leo X. Lee, also appear in "Lola," which con-stitutes the Circus part of my book Saga/Circus (Omnidawn, 2008). Time has gone by since the circus. Leo X. Lee is still (as I described him in my working notes) a "fidgety musician," but Maggie Fornetti, who was a PhD student, is now an aca-demic in a large university, and Askari Nate Martin has left the police force (homicide division) and is now the director of a city-funded program for at-risk youth called the Oakland MAP (or Oakland Music and Arts Program). Askari Nate Martin and Maggie Fornetti are now a couple with three children (Jonah Giacomo Martin, age 10; Francesca Malaya Martin, age 12 and known as "Malaya"; Antonia Alice Martin, age 6). These are changes, but they do not contribute to any plot. They shape scenarios, contrive circumstances, mean little except that time is going by—somewhere, everywhere.

Time, meanwhile, is crowded with the doings of human life, at least for humans. And it is thick with contingencies and chance occurrences, but also with the overlooked, misunder-stood, maltreated. Positions is, I hope, about political activism and its aesthetic corollary in intellectual and in everyday life, which I continue to value as interrelated and reciprocally inform-ing spheres.

Notes

All comments that appear without quotation marks and are attributed to real people in the text, if not cited below, were not, in fact, said by those people.

1

"designates a presence to the plurality...": Michel de Certeau, The Practice of Everyday Life, trans. by Steven F. Rendall (Berkeley: University of California Press, 1984), 218, fn 7.

"such an imperious need...": Jonathan Beecher, Charles Fourier: The Visionary and His World (Berkeley, Los Angeles, and London: University of California Press, 1986), 227.

"'Sleep,' as Victor Hugo has said...: Victor Hugo, The Toilers of the Sea, no translation credit (New York: Harper and Brothers, 1867, in Michigan Historical Reprint Series), 14.

"This sweeps past the mind...": Victor Hugo, Les Misérables, trans. by Lee Fahnestock and Norman MacAfee (NY: Signet Classics, 1987), 989.

It is / immune to exegesis...: Mark McMorris, "Dear Michael (16)," in Entrepôt (Coffee House, 2010), 98.

2

"From that moment onward, our loathsome society rushed...": Quoted in Walter Benjamin, The Arcades Project, trans. by Howard Eiland and Kevin McLaughlin (Cambridge and London: Belknap Press of Harvard University Press, 1999), 691.

"the paratactic revolt against synthesis...": Theodor W. Adorno, "Parataxis; On Hölderlin's Late Poetry," in Notes to Literature, volume two; trans. by Shierry Weber Nicholsen (New York: Columbia University Press, 1992), 136.

oneitd , crine / mend zin: P. Inman, Ocker (Berkeley: Tuumba Press, 1982), unpaginated; first poem.

masterpieces "exist because they came to be...": Gertrude Stein, "What Are Masterpieces," in Catherine R. Stimpson and Harriet Chessman, eds., Gertrude Stein Writings 1932-1946 (New York: Library of America, 1998), 358.

"The lovers are deeply convinced... '; "Romantic love manifests itself...": Soren Kierkegaard, Either/Or, Part 2, ed. and trans. by Howard V. Hong and Edna H. Hong (Princeton: Princeton University Press, 1987), 21.

What does one do with the excitement one feels: See Charles Altieri, The Particulars of Rapture (Ithaca and London: Cornell University Press, 2003), 167.

3

"merge tracelessly into the totality": See Theodor Adorno, Aesthetic Theory, trans. by Robert Hullot-Kentor (Minneapolis: University of Minnesota Press, 1997), 303.

The allegorical can be viewed: Thanks to Ted Alexander, who, during a fall 2010 graduate seminar discussion of Walter Benjamin's notion of allegory, noted allegory's paradoxical relationship to continuity and discontinuity, homogeneity and heterogeneity.

"If men learn this, it will implant forgetfulness...": Plato, Phaedrus 275 a-b.

"We realize in retrospect...": Charles Altieri, The Particulars of Rapture, 220.

5

"'What regiment is your son with?'...": Sigmund Freud, The Psychopathology of Everyday Life; James Strachey, ed., trans. by Alan Tyson (New York & London: W. W. Norton & Company, 1960), 71.

"I entered a house and offered my right hand...": Ibid, 176.

a "superfluity...of causes, the profusion of causes...": Elizabeth Grosz, "Becoming...An Introduction," in Elizabeth Grosz, ed., Becomings: Explorations in Time, Memory, and Futures (Ithaca: Cornell University Press, 1999), 4.

"Not to notice the accouterments...": Edward S. Casey, "The Time of the Glance," in Elizabeth Grosz, ed., Becomings, 80-81.

"[I]n the end there is no goal...": Rüdiger Safranski, Nietzsche: A Philosophical Biography, trans. by Shelley Frisch (NY: W.W. Norton & Co, 2002), 115.

6

"to face with heroic composure": Walter Benjamin, The Arcades Project, 337.

"the axiom that there is no such thing...": Letters of Gustave Flaubert 1830–1857, Francis Steegmuller, ed. (Cambridge, MA: Harvard University Press, 1980), 154.

"[Flaubert] forced me to describe...": Quoted in Graham Robb, "Cruising with Genius," in The New York Review of Books, Feb. 26, 2009, 33-34.

"[T]he true object of anxiety...": Slavoj Žižek, Welcome to the Desert of the Real (London and NY: Verso, 2002), 22.

There are countless ways to combine existences: See de Certeau, 21.

"I don't know how it is, unless it's on account of being stupid...": Charles Dickens, David Copperfield, Chapter VIII: "My Holidays, Especially One Happy Afternoon".

"So we appeal to you, sun...": John Ashbery, Girls on the Run (New York: Farrar, Straus and Giroux, 1999), 9.

7

"Everyday life is the supreme court...": Henri Lefebvre, Critique of Everyday Life, vol. 1; trans. John Moore (London: Verso, 2008), 6.

"from the flowers of a variety of unrelated plants": thanks to John Wilkinson for pointing out the definition of polylectic; see http://en.wiktionary.org/wiki/polylectic

"Sounds penetrate partitions...": Lucretius, On the Nature of Things; trans. and notes by Martin Ferguson Smith (Indianapolis: Hackett Publishing Company, Inc., 2001), 12.

"The mouth that tells not will ever attract the unthinking tongue....": James Joyce, Finnegans Wake, 68.

"There... emerges a... possibility...": Fredric Jameson, Postmodernism, or, the Cultural Logic of Late Capitalism (Durham, NC: Duke University Press, 1991), 394.

"Postmodernism found itself in a world of multiple cultures...": A paraphrase of comments he made in a University of California, Berkeley class lecture on J.M. Coetzee's Disgrace, UC Berkeley, November 26, 2012.

"For some time I used to carry a stick...": Sigmund Freud, The Psychopathology of Everyday Life, 170.

"ambiguity is a category of everyday life...": Lefebvre, Critique of Everyday Life, vol. 1, 18.

"History reads the past...": Peter Bürger, The Theory of the Avant-Garde; trans. by Michael Shaw, (University of Minnesota Press, 1984), 21.

the young Arthur Conan Doyle in his diary: Arthur Conan Doyle, "Dangerous Work": Diary of an Arctic Adventure (Chicago, University of Chicago Press, 2012), 276, 293. Doyle's Sherlock Holmes character will devote his reasoning powers to finding pathways back again from metaphor to fact.

"The metaphor is...the originary form...": Ernesto Grassi, Rhetoric as Philosophy: The Humanist Tradition, trans. by Timothy W. Crusius (Carbondale IL: Southern Illinois University Press, 1980), 7; quoted in Christopher D. Johnson, Memory, Metaphor, and Aby Warburg's Atlas of Images (Ithaca, NY: Cornell University Press, 2012), 44.

"one detects creative power by its capacity...": Marianne Moore, "The Labors of Hercules," in Complete Poems (NY: The Macmillan Company / The Viking Press, 1967), 53.

8

as Arthur Symons put it: Arthur Symons, The Symbolist Movement in Literature (London: William Heinemann, 1899), 138.

"How, then, can the aesthetic...": Kierkegaard, 133.

everyday life "absolutely defeats being represented...": Michael Fried, Menzel's Realism: Art and Embodiment in Nineteenth-Century Berlin (New Haven: Yale University Press, 2002), 147.

"symbolism and praxis cannot be separated": Henri Lefebvre, The Production of Space (Cambridge, MA: Basil Blackwell, 1991), 193.

"whatever exists must be something...": Lucretius, On the Nature of Things; trans. and notes by Martin Ferguson Smith (Indianapolis: Hackett Publishing Company, Inc., 2001), 14.

9

"One protests," he says, "in order to save...": John Berger, Bento's Sketchbook, 79.

"You want to satisfy the hunger...": Kierkegaard, 160-61.

"If he indeed conceived of consciousness...": Rita Burnham, "Intelligent Seeing," in Pierre Bonnard: The Late Still Lifes and Interiors (New York: The Metropolitan Museum of Art and New Haven: Yale University Press, 2009), 72.

"Beauty demands the present...": Charles Altieri, The Particulars of Rapture, 200.

"Even the lowliest of individuals...": Kierkegaard, 175.

10

"The madman does not notice...": Diderot's Letters to Sophie Volland, selected and trans. by Peter France (London: Oxford University Press, 1972), 85-86.

"like what Nietzsche called 'lightning flashes,'...": Martin Jay, "Historical Explanation and the Event: Reflections on the Limits of Contextualization," in New Literary History 42 (2011), 564.

"We are too much like oysters...": Herman Melville, Moby-Dick; Chapter 7, "The Chapel"

"In this day and age, everyday life is lit...": Henri Lefebvre, "The Theory of Moments," in Critique of Everyday Life, vol. 2, 348.

"the space of confrontation between the sign...": Rosalind Krauss, "Notes on the Index: Seventies Art in America," October 3 (Spring 1977), 152.

"a proposition [...] is an offer...": Barbara Maria Stafford, Visual Analogy: Consciousness as the Art of Connecting (Cambridge, MA: MIT Press, 1999), 183.

"Who comes is occupied": George Oppen, New Collected Poems, ed. Michael Davidson (NY: New Directions, 2002), 14.

"gain a history": See Kierkegaard, 250.

"The clock was striking. The leaden circles...": Virginian Woolf, Mrs. Dalloway (NY: Harcourt, 1981), 186.

"He could not simply tell them...": War and Peace, trans. by Richard Pevear and Larisa Volokhonsky (NY: Alfred A. Knopf, 2007), 242.

11
"The idea of happiness continues...": Detlev Clausen, Theodor W. Adorno: One Last Genius, trans. by Rodney Livingstone (Cambridge, MA: Harvard University Press, 2008), 43.

"For all reification is forgetting...": Theodor Adorno and Walter Benjamin, The Complete Correspondence 1928-1940, ed. Henri Lonitz, trans. by Nicholas Walker (Cambridge, MA: Harvard University Press, 1999), 321.

"Flies seem to experience...": Isabelle Stengers, Thinking With Whitehead, trans. by Michael Chase (Cambridge, MA: Harvard University Press, 2011), 66.

12
"The earth moves on from day to night...": Arthur Schopenhauer, The World as Will and Representation, vol. 1, Dover, 281.

Allen Grossman has argued that perspective: Allen Grossman, in a short seminar on Willliam Blake, presented in October 2001 at the University of Utah, Salt Lake City.

13
"Without my swearing to it...": Miguel de Cervantes, Don Quixote, trans. by Edith Grossman (NY: HarperCollins, 2003), 3.

"Steel-blue and light, ruffled...": Hermann Broch, The Death of Virgil, trans. by Jean Starr Untermeyer (San Francisco: North Point Press, 1983), 11.

"To the child...": Broch, 435.

"Art itself is constructed...": Viktor Shklovsky, Energy of Delusion, trans. by Shushan Avagyan (Champaign, IL: Dalkey Archive Press, 2007), 427.

"That's been the old philosophical injunction...": Jacques Derrida, Learning to Live Finally, trans. by Pascale-Anne Brault and Michael Noas (Hoboken, NJ: Melville House Publishing, 2007), 24.

"Having before him a four-month wait...": Walter Benjamin, quoting Charles-M. Limousin, The Arcades Project, 621.

"capriciousness of meaning": Susan Buck-Morss, The Dialectics of Seeing (Cambridge, MA: MIT Press, 1991), 55.

"In everything else there may be sham...": Michel de Montaigne, in The Complete Works of Michel de Montaigne, trans. by Donald Frame (Stanford, California: Stanford University Press, 1957), 54-55.

"The vibrancy of collective fantasy...": Buck-Morss, 29.

"conceptual centers": Buck-Morss, 56.

14
"the growing uneventfulness of modernity": Christa Wolf, One Day a Year: 1960-2000; trans. by Lowell A. Baengarter (NY: Europa Editions, 2003), 497.

"It seems that in order to have a new society...": Viktor Shklovsky, Energy of Delusion: A Book on Plot, trans. by Sushan Avagyan (Champaign, IL: Dalkey Archive Press, 2007), 350.

"These details, which are incorrectly termed little...": Les Misérables, 119.

"What would art be, as the writing of history...": Adorno, Aesthetic Theory, 261.

"art reaches toward reality...": Theodor W. Adorno, Aesthetic Theory, 286.

"remarkable propensity for structures...": Walter Benjamin, 126.

15
"A few constellations here and there...": Les Misérables, 870, 905.

"Living in a society means learning...": Stafford, 131.

"The only way to remember a place...": G.K. Chesterton, Charles Dickens (Cornwall, UK: House of Stratus, 2001), 20.

a "turn to ordinariness" and producing "thick descriptions": See Martin Jay, Songs of Experience: Modern American and European Variations on a Universal Theme (Berkeley: University of California Press, 2005), 242-43.

what E.P. Thompson termed "history from below": E. P. Thompson, "History from Below," Times Literary Supplement, 7 April 1966, pp. 279–80.

Jean Millet is said to have once remarked: T.J. Clark, The Absolute Bourgeois: Artists and Politics in France 1848-1851 (Berkeley: University of California Press, 1973), 94.

16
"Hope, or utopian desire...": Carla Harryman, letter to the co-authors of The Grand Piano: An Experiment in Collective Autobiography, 1975-1980, parts 1-X (Detroit: Mode A, 2006-10), sent via email to grandpiano@lists.wayne.edu, Aug 16, 2011.

"What you are able to construct in language...": Fredric Jameson, Late Marxism (London & New York: Verso, 2007), 11.

"Something stirred on a cold night...": From an unpublished story by Diego Hurtado.

I am omnipresent to some extent: "B," first published in From the Sustaining Air (Majorca: Divers Press, 1953); reprinted in Curtis Faville and Robert Grenier, eds., The Collected Poems of Larry Eigner, vol. 1 (Stanford: Stanford University Press, 2010), 66.

"that the paternalistic control imposed...": David Hayman, "'The Pilsener Had the Baar': HCE's Sorry Case" Papers on Joyce 1 (1995), 8.

"'so be it': the ultimate expression...": Charles Altieri, The Particulars of Rapture, 137.

what Ato Quayson terms "inexorable sequentiality": Ato Quayson, Calibrations: Reading for the Social (Minneapolis: University of Minnesota Press, 2003), xvii.

the feelings one aspires to keep available: This comment, and many others in this work pertaining to affective values and their importance to aesthetic experience, are deeply indebted to Charles Altieri's immensely important writings on art and affect. See especially The Particulars of Rapture.

"systems are pictured as relatively autonomous...": J. LaPlanche and J.-B. Pontalis, The Language of Psycho-Analysis, trans. by Donald Nicholson-Smith (New York and London: W. W. Norton & Company, 1973), 452.

17
"Through violations of the orthodoxy...": Theodor Adorno, "The Essay as Form," in Notes to Literature, vol. 1, trans. by Shierry Weber Nicholsen (NY: Columbia University Press, 1991), 23.
"When you read a book, sir...": Xavier de Maistre, A Journey Around My Room, trans. by Andrew Brown (Hesperus Classics, 2004), 12.
"It was a great victory back then...": subtitle copied from Strike (in Polish Strajk), directed by Volker Schlöndorff.
"I pity you, unhappy stars...": Goethe, "Night Thoughts"
"life, extended through art": Viktor Shklovsky, Energy of Delusion, 358.
"The increase of men...": Victor Hugo, quoted in The Arcades Project, 286.
"The great god Pan is dead": Plutarch, De defectu oraculorum (The Obsolescence of Oracles), in Moralia, 5:17.

18
"It is an argument of self-assertion...": Renato Poggioli, The Theory of the Avant-Garde (Cambridge, MA: Harvard University Press, 1968), 4.
Mikhail Epstein has proposed: See Mikhail Epstein, PreDictionary (Berkeley: Atelos, 2011) or www.emory.edu/INTELNET/index.html.
"Not even men well versed in affairs...": Quoted in Michael Della Rocca, Spinoza (London

and NY: Routledge, 2008), 218; Della Rocca doesn't make clear whether the quote is from the Tractatus Politicus or the Tractatus Theologico-Politicus.
"I thought that if I could put it all down...": John Ashbery, "The New Spirit," in Three Poems (NY: The Viking Press, 1972), 3.
"trusted brutal transitions...": Stengers, 120.
"The nursery governor flew...": Thomas MacGreevy, "Homage to Hieronymus Bosch," in Keith Tuma, ed., Anthology of Twentieth-Century British & Irish Poetry (New York and Oxford: Oxford University Press, 2001), 199-201.
"Not one of the so-called rights of man...": Karl Marx, "On the Jewish Question," in Early Writings, trans. by Rodney Livingstone and Gregor Benton (New York: Vintage Books, 1975), 230-31.
"The human spirit begins to accustom...": Quoted in Walter Benjamin, The Arcades Project, 176.
"We try all the ways...": Montaigne, 815.

19
"attract the beholder...": Michael Fried, Absorption and Theatricality (Chicago: Chicago University Press, 1980), 92; quoted in W.J.T. Mitchell, What Do Pictures Want?: The Lives and Loves of Images (Chicago, University of Chicago Press, 2005), 36.
"permanently delaying —— even foiling —— ...": Jack Flam, "Bonnard in the History of Twentieth-Century Art," in Dita Amory, ed., Pierre Bonnard: The Late Still Lifes and Interiors (NY: Metropolitan Museum of Art and New Haven: Yale University Press, 2009), 55.

"quality of passage": Alfred North Whitehead, The Concept of Nature (Cambridge, UK: Cambridge University Press, 1964), 55 ——— quoted in Stengers, 56.

"Though the sun always shines literally...": Thomas Leddy, "Sparkle and Shine," in British Journal of Aesthetics 37 (July 1997).

"a diabolic enigmatic gaiety": Les Misérables, 994–95.

20

Charlie Altieri speaks of "the muted but persistent pain...": Charles Altieri, Wallace Stevens and the Demands of Modernity: Toward a Phenomenology of Value (Ithaca, NY: Cornell University Press, 2013), 191.

W. J. T. Mitchell speaks of "'lost objects'...": What Do Pictures Want?, 121.

Coleridge's wife, "dear Sara": Coleridge's own account of the injury can be found in a letter to Robert Southey dated July 17, 1787; my thanks to Claire Marie Stancek for calling this letter to my attention.

"Heat is the consequence of light...": Ron Silliman, The Alphabet (Tuscaloosa, Alabama: University of Alabama Press, 2008), 459.

"Every day for one year I looked...": Ron Silliman, The Alphabet, 1060.

what Manuel De Landa calls "a flexible behavioral repertoire": Manuel De Landa, "Deleuze, Diagrams, and the Open-Ended Becoming," in Elizabeth Grosz, ed., Becomings, 36.

But maybe Things should be loved: Vladimir Mayakovsky, "Vladimir Mayakovsky, A Tragedy," trans. by Guy Daniels; quoted in Viktor Shklovsky, A Hunt for

Optimism; trans. by Shushan Avagyan (Champaign, IL: Dalkey Archive Press, 2012), 107.

21

"The lantern is Death...": Quoted in T. J. Clark, Picasso and Truth: From Cubism to Guernica (Princeton & Oxford: Princeton University Press, 2013), 248.

"the best way to true happiness...": Leo Tolstoy, in R.F. Christian, ed. and trans., Tolstoy's Diaries (London: Flamingo, 1994), 100.

"[W]ildness and otherness are always just there...": T. J. Clark, Picasso and Truth, 145.

"To happiness the same applies as to truth...": Theodor Adorno, Minima Moralia, 112.

"[I]n the mode of everydayness...": Michael Fried, Menzel's Realism, 173-4.

22

"The moving about that the city multiplies...": Michel de Certeau, 103.

it is thin, our cynicism: Sean Bonney, Happiness: Poems After Rimbaud (London, UK: Unkant Publishing, 2011), 14.

"The conveyance of some sense-objects...": Isabelle Stengers, 89.

every possible combination: Sean Bonney, Happiness, 14.

"the feeling," as Angus Fletcher notes: Angus Fletcher, Allegory: The Theory of a Symbolic Mode (Princeton: Princeton University Press, 2012; reprint of 1964 edition), 183.

"allegory always demonstrates...": Angus Fletcher, Allegory, 303.

"One of the strongest proofs of the irrationality...": Pierre-Francois Moreau, "Fortune and the Theory of History," in Warren Montag and Ted Stolze, eds., The New Spinoza (Minnesota University Press, 1997), 98.

"The wren goes to 't...": Maynard Mack, Alexander Pope: A Life (NY and London: W. W. Norton & Co., in association with New Haven ad London: Yale University Press, 1985), 293.

"the unbearable realism of a dream": G.K. Chesterton, Charles Dickens, 20.

23

"The success of the imaginative experiment...": Alfred North Whitehead, Process and Reality (Corrected Edition); David Ray Griffin and Donald W. Sherburne, eds. (NY: The Free Press, 1978), 5.

A permanent sense of permanent alterity: See Julia Kristeva, Hannah Arendt (NY: Columbia Univ. Press, 2001), 37.

"early on the morning of 5 August 1676...": Svetlana Alpers, The Art of Describing: Dutch Art in the Seventeenth Century (University of Chicago Press, 1983), 127-8.

"[W]e should investigate the underside...": Norbert Guterman and Henri Lefebvre, La Conscience mystifiée (1936), quoted in Walter Benjamin, The Arcades Project, 765.

"Heat is the element that predominates...": Lucretius, On the Nature of Things, 75.

"There's a sermon now...": Moby-Dick, 1256.

"Nothing can be added to history...:" Watten, Constructivist Moment, 223.

24

Having a capacity for grammar: See Dorion Sagan, "Introduction" to Jacob von Uesküll, A Foray into the Worlds of Animals and Humans (original German publication, 1934; Minneapolis: University of Minnesota Press, 2010).

"If you abolish the whole...": Alfred North Whitehead, Process and Reality, Corrected Edition, David Ray Griffin and Donald W. Sherburne, eds. (New York: The Free Press, 1978) 288.

"The stars have [...] virtue...": Angus Fletcher, Allegory, 96.

25

"Death does not destroy things...": Lucretius, On the Nature of Things, 60.

"Tacit knowing is built up over time...": Patricia von Bonsdorff, "Building and the Naturally Unplanned," in The Aesthetics of Everyday Life, 82.

26

"a stupid and monstrous ornament": Montaigne, 6.

"No chain is homogeneous...": Deleuze & Guattari, Anti-Oedipus, 39.

Elizabeth Grosz, writing on the threshold of a new millennium: Elizabeth Grosz, "Becoming...An Introduction," in Elizabeth Grosz, ed., Becomings, 8, 10.

"During the day I was sustained...": Viktor Frankenstein, 201-202.

Coda

"Each generation must discover its mission...": Frantz Fanon, The Wretched of the Earth; trans. by Richard Philcox (New York: Grove Press, 2004), 145.

"I loathed it all...": Simone de Beauvoir, The Force of Circumstance, Vol II: The Autobiography of Simone de Beauvoir, trans. by Peter Green

(NY: Paragon House, 1992), 321;
quoted in "Foreword: Framing
Fanon," in Fritz Fanon, The
Wretched of the Earth, xxxiii–iv.

"Who are the most
despicable creatures?": Isobel
Grundy, ed., Lady Mary Wortley
Montagu, Selected Letters (New
York and London: Penguin Books,
1997), 463.

"If I stop to describe the
present...": Milli Graffi in A
Megaphone, Juliana Spahr and
Stephanie Young, eds., 107.

"I cannot part without
regret from the stick...": Xavier de
Maistre, A Nocturnal Expedition
Around My Room; no translation
credit (Charleston, SC: Nabu Press,
2010; a photocopy of an early
English language edition of the
1794 French edition)

"We have to learn to think
differently...": Friedrich Nietzsche,
Daybreak; Maudemarie Clark
and Brian Leiter, eds.; trans. by
R.J. Hollingdale (Cambridge, UK:
Cambridge University Press, 1997),
103.

Not in Utopia ——— [...]:
William Wordsworth, The Prelude,
10: 723–27.

Afterword
"study is what you do with
    other people....": Stefano
    Harney and Fred Moten, The
    Undercommons: Fugitive
    Planning & Black Study (New
    York: Minor Compositions,
    2013), 110.

Acknowledgements

My thanks to Marka Ellertson for advising me as to contemporary youth vernacular.

1
Published under the title "Tiring Life" in Conversations at the Wartime Café, edited by Sean Labrador y Manzano (San Francisco: McSweeney's, 2011).

2
Published in LitHub, edited by Blair Beusman and Adam Fitzgerald, July 5, 2018, https://lithub.com/.

3
Published under the title "I can't concentrate for long" in Axon: Creative Explorations, vol. 4, no. 2, edited by Jessica L. Wilkinson and Ali Alizadeh, Dec. 2014, www. axonjournal.com.au.

4
Published in The Elders Series #5 (Brooklyn: Belladonna* Collaborative, 2009).

5
Published under the title "Sun and Necessity" in Floor, no. 1, edited by Christopher Patrick Miller and Lyn Hejinian, Feb. 12, 2012, floorjournal.com.

6
Appeared under the title "City Under Sun" in the "Urban Arias" issue of Conjunctions, no. 55, edited by Bradford Morrow, Fall 2010.

7
Portion, here revised, published in The Idea of the Avant Garde— And What It Means Today, edited by Marc James Léger (Manchester, UK: Manchester University Press, 2014).

8
Appeared under the title "Live Call Allegory: For Real" in Some Pigeons are More Equal Than Others, edited by Julius von Bismarck, Julian Charriere, and Eric Ellingsen (Zurich: Lars Müller Publishers, 2015).

9
Published under the title "Noting Nothing" in Vlak, vol. 5, edited by Louis Armand.

10
Published under the title "The Maddening of Connections," in Armed Cell, vol. 3, edited by Brian Ang (spring 2012).

11
Under the title "My Silence a Name," in Conversations at a Wartime Café, vol. 2, edited by Sean Labrador y Manzano.

12
Under the title "Epithet," published in Maggy, edited by Adam Fitzgerald.

13
Appeared under the title "The Shifting Position of the Sun" in Kulturo: Sociale Fantasier, no. 29, Aug. 2009 (Copenhagen, Denmark).

14
Under the title "Children Love Color" in The Elders Series #5 (Brooklyn: Belladonna* Collaborative, 2009) and in Conjunctions, vol. 58, "Riveting: The Obsession Issue" (spring 2012).

15
Appeared under the title "The Peripheral Position of the Sun" in Plume, edited by Danny Lawless, Sept. 2012, plumepoetry.com.

16
"A Small Theory," in FPC (Formes Poetiques Contemporaines) edited by Vincent Broqua and Jean-Jacques Poucel (Presses Universitaires du Nouveau Monde, 2012).

17
Published in The Elders Series #5 (Brooklyn: Belladonna* Collaborative, 2009) and in Poetry International, no. 20/21, edited by Ilya Kaminsky (2015).

18
Published under the title "Sun on the Avant-Garde" in The Force of What's Possible: Writers on Accessibility & the Avant-Garde, edited by Lily Hoang and Joshua Marie Wilkinson (New York: Nightboat Books, 2014).

19
Unpublished; on "A Phenomenological Face"; dedicated to Charles Altieri.

20
Published under the title "Tacit knowledge" in Mantis, no. 12, edited by Chiyuma Elliott.

21
Published as "Turbulent thinking" in Journal of Poetics Research, edited by John Tranter (Sydney, Australia): http://poeticsresearch. com/?article=lyn-hejinian-turbulent-thinking.

22
Unpublished.

23
Unpublished.

24
Published as "One Poem by Lyn Hejinian" on Hyperallergic, edited by Wendy Xu, June 6, 2018, https://hyperallergic.com/445870/ one-poem-by-lyn-hejinian/.

25
Unpublished.

26
Published under the title "From Positions of the Sun" in the PEN Poetry Series, edited by Danniel Schoonebeek, June 13, 2018, https://pen.org/ from-positions-of-the-sun/.

CODA
Unpublished.

Positions of the Sun
Lyn Hejinian

Copyright © 2018 Lyn Hejinian
ISBN: 978-0-9988439-0-2
Designed by Jack Henrie Fisher

Belladonna* is a reading and
publication series that promotes
the work of women writers who
are adventurous, experimental,
politically involved, multiform,
multicultural, multi-gendered,
impossible to define, delicious
to talk about, unpredictable, &
dangerous with language.

This book has been made possible
in part by the New York State
Council on the Arts, the Leslie
Scalapino - O Books Fund, the
National Endowment for the Arts,
and donations from individuals.
Belladonna* is a proud member of
CLMP.

Library of Congress Cataloging-in-
Publication Data

Names: Hejinian, Lyn, author.
Title: Positions of the sun /
Lyn Hejinian. Description: First
edition. | Brooklyn, New York :
Belladonna Collaborative, 2018.

Identifiers: LCCN 2017034067 |
ISBN 9780998843902 (softcover :
acid-free paper)
Classification: LCC PS3558.E4735
A6 2018 | DDC 814/.54--dc23
LC record available at https://lccn.
loc.gov/2017034067

distributed to the trade by
Small Press Distribution
1341 Seventh Street
Berkeley, CA 94710
spdbooks.org

also available directly through
Belladonna* Collaborative
925 Bergen Street, Suite 405
Brooklyn, NY 11238
belladonnaseries.org

*deadly nightshade, a cardiac
and respiratory stimulant, having
purplish-red flowers and black
berries.